STO

E\

Welcome to Stockholm!

This opening fold-out contains a general map of Stockholm to help you visualise the six large districts discussed in this guide, and four pages of valuable information, handy tips and useful addresses.

Discover Stockholm through six districts and six maps

A Gamla stan
B Nybroplan / Blasieholmen / Skeppsholmen
C City / Norrmalm / Kungsholmen
D Östermalm
E Djurgården
F Södermalm

For each district there is a double-page of addresses (restaurants – listed in ascending order of price – cafés, bars, tearooms, music venues and shops), followed by a fold-out map for the relevant area with the essential places to see (indicated on the map by a star ★). These places are by no means all that Stockholm has to offer, but to us they are unmissable. The grid-referencing system (**A** B2) makes it easy for you to pinpoint addresses quickly on the map.

Transportation and hotels in Stockholm

The last fold-out consists of a transportation map and four pages of practical information that include a selection of hotels.

Index

Lists all the street names, sites and monuments featured in this guide.

Welcome to Stockholm!

A Gamla stan
B Nybroplan / Blasieholmen / Skeppsholmen
C City / Norrmalm / Kungsholmen

D Östermalm
E Djurgården
F Södermalm

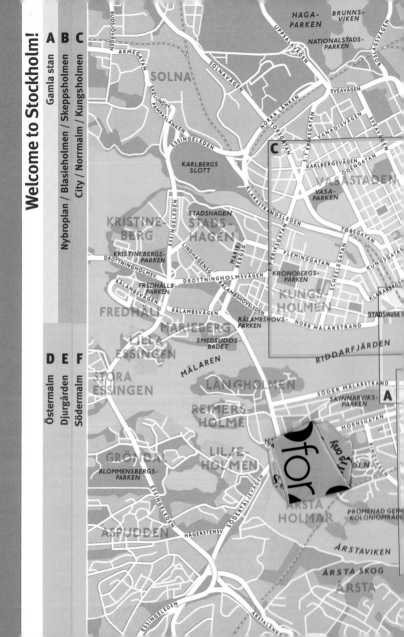

SÖDER MÄLARSTRAND

SÖDER MÄLAR

SÖDER KNUTSSONSGATAN

MARIABERGET

MARIABERGET

MONTELIUSVÄGEN

PRYS

4

TORKEL KNUTSSONSGATAN

TIMMERMANSGATAN

BELLMANS

IVAR LOS PARK

BASTUGATAN

IVAR LO-MUSEET

BLECKTORNSGRÄND

SÖ

LUDVIGSBERGSG.

TAVASTGATAN

EBENESER-
KYRKAN

GAMLA LUNDAG

A

B

C

BRÄNDA TOMTEN

MÅRTEN TROTZIGS GRÄND

RIDDARHUSET

★ **Medeltidsmuseet**
(**A** E1)
→ *Norrbro; Tel. 508 31 790
Closed until 2010, but
temporary exhibition at the
Kulturhuset* (**C** D3)
The award-winning museum
of medieval Stockholm
depicts the origins and
early history of the city up
to the Middle Ages, through
imaginative reconstructions
of a whole district, with its
streets, harbor and gallows
hill. Fascinating.

★ **Kungliga slottet** (**A** E2)
→ *Tel. 402 61 30
Mid-May-mid-Sep: daily
10am-4pm (5pm June-Aug);
mid-Sep-mid-May: Tue-Sun
noon-3pm; closed three
weeks in Jan*

Destroyed by fire in 1697,
the Royal Palace was rebuilt
in 1754 by architect
Nicodemus Tessin the
Younger in the form of a
baroque Italian palazzo.
Behind its Renaissance
façade are over 600 rooms
designed in a mixture of
rococo and classical styles.
Grand receptions are held
here as it is the official
residence of the royal
family, though the latter
prefers staying at
Drottningholm.
Livrustkammaren
(Royal Armory)
A display of royal history:
armor and armory, coaches,
coronation regalia, wedding
dresses and even a stuffed

horse, the favorite toy of
young Gustavus II Adolphus
(1611–32).
The Guest Apartments
The sumptuous interiors
date from the 18th and
19th centuries.
Slottsmuseet Tre Kronor
(Kronor Museum)
Insight into daily life at
court from the 13th to the
17th centuries.
Skattkammaren (Treasury)
Kept in the vaulted cellar
below the Throne Room:
the Crown Jewels include
the key, the sword of state,
the scepter and the orb.
Vaktavlösning (Changing
of the Guard)
→ *Tel. 402 63 17
June-Aug: Mon-Sat 12.15pm;*

*Sun and public hols 1
Oct-April: Wed-Sat 12.
Sun and public hols 1.
Duration: 15 mins*
Spectacular parade
courtyard of the pal
the royal guards ma
in their blue uniform
gleaming helmets t
sound of a military b
★ **Storkyrkan** (**A** [
→ *Trångsund 1
Tel. 723 30 00 21 Dai
9am-6pm (4pm Oct-A*
Despite its beautifu
baroque façade, the
brick Stockholm Ca
(1279) remains a Go
jewel. It houses pric
treasures, such as th
15th-century *St Geor
and the Danish Drago*

A

MP MACKOR

GN AT 125 KVADRAT

VAKHOLM

THE ARCHIPELAGO

→ *Ferries from Nybrokajen (B A1) and Strömkajen (B A2); guided tours: May-Sep*
Stockholm's unique archipelago is made of 24,000 islands and islets, stretching 50 miles east of the city. Among them the idyllic **Vaxholm**, renowned for its beaches, fortress, lovely wooden houses and boutiques; **Grinda**, for swimming in crystal clear waters; **Finnhamn**, for hikes in the beautifully preserved natural landscape; and **Sandhamn**, known for its summer regattas and beautiful beaches.

ING OUT

oms

kfast (sweet and ry) is usually so tantial that a snack unch in a *fik* will be ugh. All restaurants a set lunch (*meny*) veen 11am and 2pm d, main course, bread, k and coffee).
ice is very basic in ler establishments: collect your own cutlery glass before eating, read, water and e are free.
e has been a move rd fusion food, mixing tional cuisine with gn influences; such us can be expensive unusual and an eable surprise.
ing
erally included, but e 10 percent on top if were satisfied with ervice.

Eating out

Fik: cafés for light meals (*mackor*, simple dishes, sandwiches and pastries), often served buffet-style.
Konditori: bakery, cake shop and tearoom.

Swedish specialties

Gravad lax: marinated salmon;
Hjortron: wild, orange-colored berries known as cloudberries or salmon berries;
Husmanskost: traditional Swedish cookery;
Kanelbulle: cinnamon bun;
Kaviar: creamed fish roe, often in a tube;
Knäckebröd: crispbread;
Köttbullar: meatballs;
Lingon: lingon berries, like wild cranberries;
Mackor/smörgåsar: slices of bread or sandwiches, often open;
Pyttipanna: cubed meat, potatoes, onion and bacon fried together;
Renkött: reindeer meat;

Sill (inlagd sill): marinated herring;
Skorpa: grilled bread;
Smörgåsbord: traditional Swedish buffet;
Strömming: Baltic herring;
Snaps: eau-de-vie;
Ärtsoppa: pea soup with bacon, eaten on Thursdays.

GOING OUT

Program

Check out the excellent bimonthly (monthly in summer) *What's On*, available free of charge from the Sverigehuset, in youth hostels, etc.

Shows

Cheaper seats on offer at the opera one hour before the performance. Free open-air theater in summer in the city parks (Parkteatern) and concerts every evening at Kungsträdgården (**C** E3).
BiljettdirektTicnet
→ *Tel. 077 170 70 70*
www.ticnet.se
Tickets for most shows and other cultural events.

Theaters

Dramaten (**B** A1)
→ *Nybroplan*
Tel. 667 06 80 (box office)
The fabulous Royal Theater in a beautiful Art Nouveau building.
Södra Teatern (**F** C1)
→ *Mosebacke torg 1-3*
Tel. 556 972 30
The best venue for world music. Several acts each night, plus café and bar.
Folkoperan (**F** A1)
→ *Hornsg. 72; Tel. 616 07 50*
Experimental shows and productions rather than standard repertory.

Bars, nightclubs

Meet under the 'mushroom' in Stureplan Square (**C** E2) before setting off to cruise the hippest city bars. Bohemian and alternative nightspots on Götgatan in Södermalm, and in trendy SoFo.

EXCURSIONS

EXCURSIONS

Birka
→ Tel. 560 514 45
Boat from Stadshusbron
(C D4)
The trading place of the
Viking Age, and a World
Heritage site. Museum,
archeological digs...

Drottningholm
→ To Brommaplan subway
station then bus 301 & 323,
or boat from Stadshusbron;
www.dtm.se

Royal castle
Tel. 402 62 80
A late 17th-century
palace, set in a beautiful
park. The royal residence
is open to the public.

Kina slott
→ Tel. 402 62 70
Chinese pavilion, with a
collection of objets d'art
from the 18th century.

Theater
The auditorium has
remained unchanged
since it was built in 1766,
and still has the original
stage machinery. Guided
tours and performances.

Fjäderholmarna
→ Boats from
Nybrokajen **(B** A1)
and Strömkajen **(B** A2)
Islands from the city's
nearest archipelago,
with a craft village,
the Östersjö aquarium,
a boat museum,
beaches, etc.

Millesgården
→ Lidingö; Tel. 446 75 80
To Ropsten subway then
bus 207
Home and studio of
the sculptor Carl Milles
(1875–1955), a student of
Rodin, now a museum
and a sculpture park in
a terraced garden high
above Stockholm with
breathtaking views.

SHOPPING

City
Major names in prêt-à-
porter can be found on
Drottninggatan (**C** C2-3).

Department stores & malls
NK (C E3)
→ Hamngatan 18-20
Sweden's answer to
Bergdorf Goodman or
Selfridges.

Åhléns (C D3)
→ Klarabergsgatan 50
Sweden's best-known
department store.

Gallerian (C E3)
→ Hamngatan 37

Sturegallerian (C E2)
→ Stureplan
Exclusive department store,
just as the street it is on.

Hennes & Mauritz (C E3)
→ Hamngatan 22
The largest H&M in Sweden,
the home country of this
great ready-to-wear chain
of stores, founded in 1947.

IKEA (C E3)
→ Regeringsgatan 17

*Mon-Fri 11am–5pm; free
shuttle bus every hour*
The largest IKEA store in
the world.

Östermalm
Chic boutiques and
design furniture.

SoFo (on Södermalm)
Trendy second-hand
clothes and interior
decoration.

Tax-free
VAT is refunded to non-
European Union nationals.

SWEDISH DESIGN

Simplicity, style and utility,
a concept born in the late
19th century and which
reached its peak in the
1950s. Key figures include
the artist Carl Larsson and
his wife in the 19th century,
Josef Frank, Sigurd Persson,
Jonas Bohlin and Thomas
Sandell. Shops all over the
city. For the finest
examples, check out the
applied arts section in the

Nationalmuseum, Svensk
Form, Tekniska museet
and Nordiska museet.

STOCKHOLM
ANOTHER WAY

By boat
Stockholm Sightseeing
→ Tel. 587 140 20; www
.stockholmsightseeing.com

Djurgårdsbrons Sjöcafé
→ Galärvarsvägen 2, under
Djurgårdsbron (**D** C4)
Tel. 660 57 57
Bikes, rollerblades, canoes
and rowing boats to rent.

By bicycle
Stockholm City Bikes
→ Tel. 077 444 24 24
www.stockholmcitybikes.se
Bikes for rent (April-Oct)
from SL-Center. 25 kr/day.

Open-top tourist bus
City Sightseeing (C E3)
→ Gustav Adolfs torg
Tel. 587 140 20
Duration: 1 hr 30 mins,
with hop-on hop-off option
(Open Top Tours)

Gamla stan

RIDDARE

HOLMEN
RIDDAR-
JARLS
TÖRN

★ EVERT TAUBES
TERRASS

BIRGER
JARLS TÖRN

SVEA HOVRÄTT RÄTTEN

WRANGELSKA
PALATSET

Birger Jarls
torg

REGERINGS-

KAMMAR-
RÄTTEN

WRANGELSKA BACKEN

SÖDRA RIDDARHOLMS-
HAMNEN

GYMNASIEGR

ROSENKAMMAREN

TRYCKERIG

RIDDARHOLM

NORRA RIDDAR-
HOLMSHAMNEN

CENTRALBRON

NORRA JÄRNVÄGSBRON

STRÖMS-
BORG

BORGS
BRON

VASABRON

STRAND

BÅTAR TILL
DROTTNINGHOLM,
BIRKA

KLARA MÄLAR-

STADSHUSBRON

STADSHUSET

STADSHUSTORNET

Ragnar
Östbergs
plan

JÄRNVÄGS-
PARKEN

Tegel-
backen

Rödbod
torget

FR

KONST-
AKADEMIEN

JAKOBS

KARDUAN MAKARG

RÖDBOD

CITY

VASAGATAN

SÖDERSKOPPEL

CENTRAL-
STATIONEN

S. SLABBERGSSKOPPEL

KLARA SJÖRAMPEN

SERAFIMERSTRANDEN

1

2

A

B

C

MEDELTIDSMUSEET

KUNGLIGA SLOTTET

STORKYRKAN

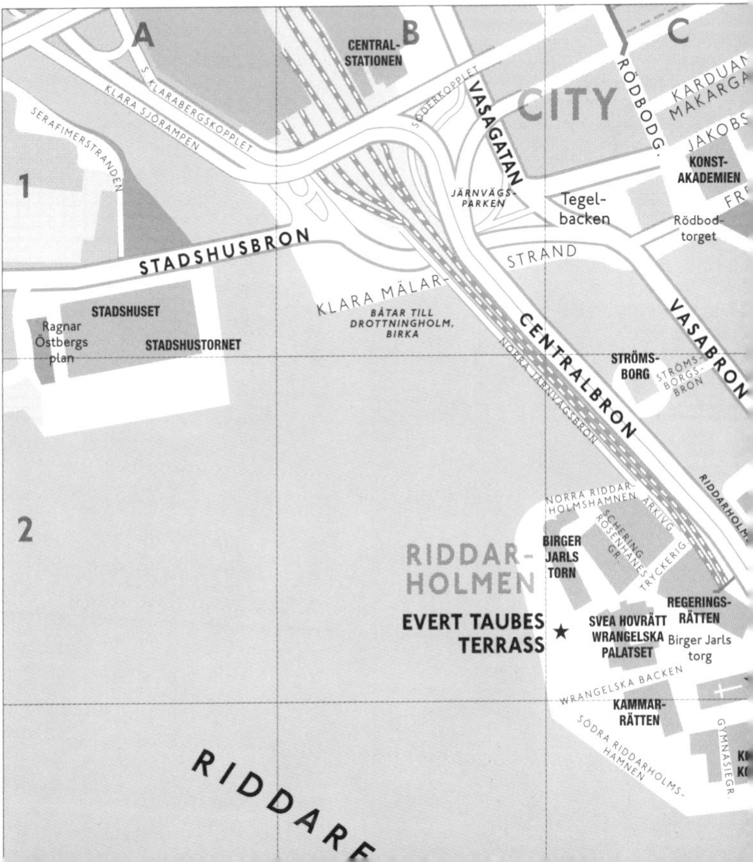

A

Gamla stan

Founded in 1255 by
Birger Jarl, the island of
Gamla stan is the historic
birthplace of Stockholm.
Its medieval decor has
many Italianate features
such as polychrome and
ocher façades, a maze of
cobbled alleyways, and
little squares like piazzas.
Tourists flock to see the
changing of the guard
ceremony outside the
magnificent Royal Palace
before exploring the
steep Västerlanggatan,
a pedestrianized street
lined with shops, and then
relaxing in one of the cafés
on the main square,
Stortorget. The churches
of Gamla stan, Gothic
and baroque in style, are
the most beautiful in
Stockholm.

If on their own the restaurant prices
given in this guide are for a main
course only.

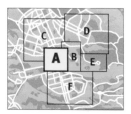

HERMITAGE

MÄLARDROTTNINGEN

RESTAURANTS

Hermitage (**A** D3)
→ Stora Nygatan 11
Tel. 411 95 00
Daily 11am–8pm (7pm Sun)
Modern, often spicy,
vegetarian food. The
menu changes on a daily
basis – Asian dishes one
day, Moroccan cuisine the
next. 85 kr.

Café Tabac (**A** E3)
→ Stora Nygatan 46
Tel. 10 15 34 Mon-Sat
10am–midnight (1am Sat);
Sun noon–midnight
A friendly spot, rather like
a Spanish bodega, with
high stools, bright mosaics
and a list of tapas as long
as your arm. Perfect for
lunch. 48–300 Kr.

**Mandus Bar
& Kök** (**A** E2)
→ Österlånggatan 7
Tel. 20 60 55; Daily 5–11pm
Trendy, informal and
popular with the gay
crowd. Unpretentious
but excellent bistro-style
cooking in a hospitable
atmosphere, which can
get extremely busy.
94–224 kr.

Mälardrottningen (**A** C3)
→ Sodra Riddarholms-
hamnen; Tel. 545 18 780
Tue-Sat 6–11pm
Moored at the quay on
Riddarholmen, Barbara
Hutton's former luxury

yacht (1924) has now bee
transformed into a good-
quality seafood restaurar
with its inside tricked out
like a galleon and fine vie
over the city. 105–235 kr;
seafood buffet 395 kr
(reservation advised).

Bistro/Grill Ruby (**A** E2
→ Österlånggatan 14
Tel. 20 60 15 Daily 5–11pm
The Bistro is a warm, cozy
French-style brasserie wit
red-colored walls; next
door, the American grill
room has a more relaxed
atmosphere. Tex-Mex in t
latter, fish in the former.
Pleasant bar, too.
150–375 kr.

**Den Gyldene
Freden** (**A** E3)
→ Österlånggatan 51
Tel. 24 97 60
Mon-Fri 5–11pm; Sat 1–11p.
(closed Mon in summer)
Den Gyldene Freden has
hardly changed since it
opened in 1722, and
famous people from the
Swedish art world have
had their regular tables
here. Dinner is served in
the dining room or in the
darkly lit vaulted cellar.
165–325 kr.

CAFÉS, BARS

Café Edenborg (**A** E3)
→ Stora Nygatan 35
Tel. 22 10 19 Mon-Fri 10am

CAFÉ EDENBORG

SUNDBERGS KONDITORI

KERSTIN ADOLPHSON

...m; Sat-Sun noon–5pm
...here's a hushed, rather
...tudious atmosphere in
...is café-bookshop, where
...terary types come to read
...hile nibbling panini or
...her light snacks.

**...undbergs
...onditori (A** E3)
→ *Järntorget 83; Daily 9am*
...0am Sat-Sun)–8pm
...ockholm's oldest
...onditori (1785) has
...tained all its old-world
...arm. The choice of
...kes is enormous, and
...ccording to the generous
...d Swedish custom of
...*tår*, your second cup is
...n the house.

...tortorget (A E2)
...wonderful spot for
...eople-watching. The
...andsome, well-preserved
...uildings make for an
...nbeatable setting, and
...e cafés with outdoor
...rraces are aplenty.

...afé Kaffekoppen
Stortorget 20
...elicious mackor and
...ood cakes.

...hokladkoppen
Stortorget 18
...is tiny gay-friendly,
...cher-painted café serves
...ood mackor and one of
...e best hot chocolates
...the city.

...afé Satir
Stortorget 2
...e fik of the Nobel

Museum. The 'Nobel' ice
cream it serves is worthy
of the gala that follows the
famous ceremony.

Café Järntorget (A E3)
→ *Västerlånggatan 81
Tel. 22 68 20 Mon-Fri 8am–
6pm; Sat-Sun 10am–10pm*
One of the best ice cream
parlors in Gamla stan. Go
for the homemade cone,
and try the saffron flavor.

Pontus by the Sea (A F3)
→ *Skeppsbrokajen,
Tullhus 2; Tel. 20 20 95
Mon-Sat 11.30am–1am;
Sun noon–11pm*
This bar-brasserie became
famous after featuring in
the first series of a
successful Swedish reality
TV show, *Baren* ('The Bar').
Very pleasant in summer
when you get a gorgeous
180° view of Strömmen
canal from the terrace.

Stampen (A D2)
→ *Stora Nyg. 5; Tel. 20 57 93
Mon-Sat 8pm–1am (2am Fri-
Sat); www.stampen.se*
Once a church, then a
pawnbroker's (hence the
name, *stampen*, 'The Nail',
and decor), and a jazz club
since 1968. Blues gigs on
Saturday afternoons.

SHOPPING

Västerlånggatan (A E3)
The commercial street of
Gamla stan, complete

with tourist traps, but
also with some authentic
craft boutiques.

Flodins Bildantikvariat
→ *Västerlånggatan 37*
Elegant engravings and
beautiful old maps.

Kerstin Adolphson
→ *Västerlånggatan 40/44
Tel. 20 17 27*
Swedish clogs of all
kinds, with cowhide
uppers, handpainted
with various designs
(flowers, ladybirds, etc),
or in plain leather.

E. Torndahl
→ *Västerlånggatan 63*
Jewelry. Fine selection of
amber from the Baltic.

Kalikå (A E3)
→ *Österlånggatan 18
Tel. 20 52 19
Mon-Sat 10am–6pm (4pm
Sat); Sun 11am–3pm*
Carefully thought-out
creative and scientific
toys and games. Soft toys
in lovely materials and
Kalikå's own trendy
toddlers' clothes.

Ekovaruhuset (A E3)
→ *Österlånggatan 28
Tel. 22 98 45 Daily 11am–
6pm (4pm Sat-Sun)*
Set in a vaulted interior
dating from 1336, this
fashionable shop only
sells organic and fair trade
products, from chocolate
and cosmetics to shoes,
jeans, lingerie or designer

T-shirts. Sister shop in
Manhattan.

Fartygsmagasinet (A E2)
→ *Österlånggatan 19
Tel. 20 93 98 Thu-Fri 11am–
6pm; Sat 11am–3pm*
Bric-a-brac and antiques
from the Seven Seas. A
monocular for the living
room, an anchor for the
garden, or perhaps a
model ship for the nursery.

Sweden Bookshop (A E2)
→ *Slottsbacken 10
Tel. 453 78 00
Mon-Fri 10am–6pm (and
Sat 11am–4pm in July-Aug)*
The bookshop of the
Swedish Institute stocks
anything related to
Sweden – from *Pippi
Longstocking* to August
Strinberg – in all major
languages. A goldmine for
anyone interested in
learning more about this
beautiful country.

**Själagårdsbodarna
(A** E3)
→ *Själagårdsgatan 7-9 (on
Brända Tomten); Tel. 20 25 00
Mon-Sat 10am–6pm (4pm
Sat); Sun 11am–5pm*
A treasure-house stuffed
with all kinds of toys and
games for the young at
heart: wooden tableware,
old posters, adorable
wicker baskets, Christmas
decorations, and old-
fashioned playthings and
trinkets of all kinds.

STORKYRKO-
SKOLAN

BRÄNDA
TOMTEN

GAMLA STAN

POST-
MUSEUM

BRUNNSGRÄND

Brunnsplan

TYSKA
KYRKAN

ÖSTERLÅNGGATAN

BAGGENSGATAN

JOHANNESGR

TYSKA
KYRKOGATAN

STORA NYG

LILLA NYGATAN

VÄSTERLÅNGGATAN

STÅLHOPPAGR

KÅKBRINKEN

SKOMAKARGATAN

SKEPPAR KARLS GR

BÅGENS GR

PEDER FREDAGSGR

SCHÖNFELDTS GR

KÅKBRINKEN

STORTORGET

Kopman-
torget

NOBELMUSEET

SJÄLAGÅRDSG

KÅLGRÄND

KÅRLEKSG

TRÅNGSUND

KÖPMANGATAN

SKRÅDDARGR

ÖSTERLÅNGGATAN

GÅSGR

SVARTMANGATAN

PRÄSTGATAN

STORA GRÅMUNKEGR

LILLA GRÅMUNKEGR

HÄLSINGEGR

IGNATII GR

KÅLGR

SÄLJEGR

BÅDGÅRDSG

STAFFAN
SASSES
GRÄND

KÅKGRÄND

FÖRSTUGR

BREDGRÄND

SKOTTGRÄND

TRÅNGSUND

NÅKANS GR

TORTHAMMARGR

SKEPPARGR

TELEGRAFGR

KARLS GR

FINSKA
KYRKAN

BÖRSEN

KÅLLARGR

MYNTKABINETTET

KUNGLIGA

STOR-
KYRKAN

SLOTTSBACKEN

SALVIIGR

TORKERKOBRINKEN

PRÅSTGATAN

LOGÅRDSTRAPPAN

2

Gustav III:s
staty

SKATTKAMMAREN

LIVRUST-
KAMMAREN

INRE
BORG-
GÅRDEN

YTTRE
BORGGÅRDEN

KUNGLIGA
SLOTTET

LEJONBACKEN

SLOTTSBACKEN

TERRASSEN

LOGÅRDEN

TRE KRONOR

SLOTTSMUSEET

S HELGEANDSHOLMSBRON

STÅLLKANALEN

RIKSDAGS-
HUSET

ANKARGRÄND

N HELGEANDSTR

RIKSDAGS-
HUSET

LANDS-
MEN

S HELGEANDSTR

SÄGERSKA
HUSET

ARVFURSTENS
PALATS

MEDELHAVS-
MUSEET

DANSMUSEET

STRÖMBRON

Riksplan

NORRBRO

MEDELTIDS-
MUSEET

NORRSTRÖM

STRÖMGATAN

Gustav
Adolfs
torg

N

NATIONAL-
MUSEUM

MUSEI-
PARKEN

SÖDRA BLASIEHOLMSHAMNEN

HOVSLAGARG

SKÅRGÅRDSBÅTAR

SIGHT-
SEEING-
BÅTAR

SÖDRA STRÖMKAJEN

Karl XII:s
torg

OPERAN

1

E

D

NOBELMUSEET

STORTORGET

RIDDARHOLMSKYRKAN

EVERT TAUBES TERRASS

piece of
vian sculpture,
ldest painting
ting Stockholm
y Jacob Elbfas.
orget (A E2)
g trading square
past, the Stortorget
rounded by
ouses dating from
and 18th centuries.
iles on the façade
use at no. 20 are
ear the names of
emen executed by
h king Christian II
e Stockholm
th of 1520.
lmuseet (A E2)
set, Stortorget
18 00
mid-Sep: daily

10am–5pm (8pm Tue);
mid-Sep–mid-May: daily
11am–5pm (8pm Tue)
Founded by the Alfred
Nobel (1833–96), this
museum devoted to the
Nobel Prize winners is
housed in the late baroque
former stock exchange
(1776). Exhibits tell you
about the laureates and
more than a century
of scientific achievements.

★ **Brända tomten** (A E3)
An elegant piazza with
ocher façades, shaded
by a large chestnut tree.
It was named Brända
tomten ('burnt ground')
after the fire which
destroyed a block of
houses here in 1728.

★ **Mårten
Trotzigs gränd** (A E3)
With 36 steps and a width
of 90 cm (35 inches), the
city's narrowest lane was
named after a German
merchant who owned two
houses here at the end of
the 16th century.

★ **Riddarhuset** (A C2)
→ Riddarhustorget 10
Tel. 723 39 90
Mon-Fri 11.30am–12.30pm
A magnificent 17th-century
baroque town house in
which the Upper House of
the Swedish parliament
continues to hold its
assemblies. The motto
'Arte et Marte' on the
façade translates as 'in the
service of art and war'.

★ **Riddarholmskyrkan**
(A C2)
→ Birger Jarls torg
Tel. 402 61 30 Daily
10am–4pm (5pm June-Aug)
Built in the 17th century
on top of a medieval
monastery, the church
houses the remains of all
the Swedish kings since
Gustav II Adolf (1611–32).
The high bell tower (1835)
is pierced like a piece of
the finest lacework.

★ **Evert Taubes
terrass** (A C2)
The bronze sculpture of
Sweden's national
troubadour (1890–1976)
stands opposite the
loveliest view of the
city hall.

BLASIEHOLMSTORG

NATIONALMUSEUM

← Map F

B

★ **Dramaten** (**B** A1)
→ *Nybroplan*
Tel. 667 06 80 (ticket office)
Tel. 665 61 00 (guided tours)
www.dramaten.se
Both classical and
contemporary works are
performed at the Royal
Dramatic Theater, or
Dramaten. Founded in 1788
by King Gustav III to give his
people a sense of national
identity, it is a magnificent
Art Nouveau building (1908)
with a remarkable and lavish
entrance hall. The two gold
statues are by Carl Milles.
★ **Hallwylska
Museet** (**B** A1)
→ *Hamngatan 4*
Tel. 519 55599
Tue–Sun 11.45am–4pm;

guided tours: Tue–Sun noon,
1pm (in English on Sun), 2pm,
3pm (and 6pm Wed)
A splendid private mansion
dating from the 19th
century, built in a mixture
of Venetian and Spanish
Renaissance styles, with a
large, eccentric collection
of art, crafts and everyday
objects. Concerts in the
courtyard in summer.
★ **Raoul Wallenbergs
torg** (**B** A1)
In Hungary at the end of
World War 2 the Swedish
citizen Raoul Wallenberg
(1912–47?) rescued
thousands of Jews from
deportation by the Nazis.
This sculpture by the Danish
artist Kirsten Ortwed was

unveiled amid great
controversy in 2000.
Opinion was split between
those who saw in it an
artistic interpretation of
Wallenberg's mission and
those who would have
preferred a more traditional
statue in such a sensitive
architectural area.
★ **Blasieholmstorg** (**B** A2)
When the square was
renovated in 1989 two
bronze horses with green
patina were selected as
decoration, copies of those
which adorn the church of
San Marco in Venice. Why?
Because the closest streets
are named Hovslagargatan
(Blacksmith St) and
Stallgatan (Stable St).

★ **Nationalmuse**
→ *Blasieholmshamr*
Tel. 519 543 00
June–Aug: Tue–Sun 11
(8pm Tue); Sep–May:
11am–5pm (8pm Tue
www.nationalmuseu
The National Muse
(1866) holds Swede
largest painting, sc
print and drawing
collections. Master
from the Renaissan
the early 19th centu
assembled by Swe
kings throughout th
centuries are on sh
of charge: parchme
furniture, works by
Scandinavian mast
(C.G. Pilo, Alexande
Anders Zorn) and E

↑ Map C

Map area

AMIRA...
AF CHAPMAN
VANDRARHEM

4 GAMLA STAN
Kopman- NYGRAND
torget
KÄLLARGRÄND
BREDGRAND
MYNTKABINETTET
TELEGRAFGR.
STÄPPA GR.
BOLLHUSGR.

AF CHAPMAN
VANDRARHEM

SKEPPSHOLMEN
★

BATTE...
PARK...

Admira...
back

VÄ...PL...
NORRA...

SLOTTS-
BACKEN

Gustav IIIs
staty

**LIVRUST-
KAMMAREN**

SKEPPSHOLMSBRON

**NATIONAL-
MUSEUM**
★

MUSEIPARKEN

MUSEIKAJEN

BLASIEHOLMEN

HOVSLAGARGATAN
SÖDRA BLASIEHOLMSHAMNEN

SKÄRGÅRDS-
BÅTAR

STRÖMBRON

NORRSTRÖM

SIGHT-
SEING-
BÅTAR

STÅLLGATAN
TEATERGATAN
BLASIEHOLMSG.

GRAND HOTEL

GRÄVGRÄND

DJURGÅRDSFÄR...

NYBROKAJEN

NYBROVIKEN

SKÄRGÅRDS-
BÅTAR

UTFLYKTS-
BÅTAR

BLASIEHOLMSTORG
★

ARS...

NYBROKAJEN 11

**KUNGSTRAD-
GÅRDEN**
ⓘ

SYNAGOGAN

**RAOUL
WALLENBERGS
TORG**
★

SANKT EUGENIA-
KYRKAN

**BERZELII
PARK**

BERNS

DRAMATEN
★

STRANDVÄGEN

ARTILLERIGATAN

VÄPNARGATAN

KUNGLIGA
HOVSTALLET

KÅ...
POST...

NÄCKSTROMS...

NYBROGATAN
HAMNGATAN

BIRGER JARLSGATAN

CHINA-
TEATERN

**HALLWYLSKA
MUSEET**
★

Nybroplan

Norr-
malms-
torg.

NYBROG.
DRAMATEN
★

ALMLOFSGATAN

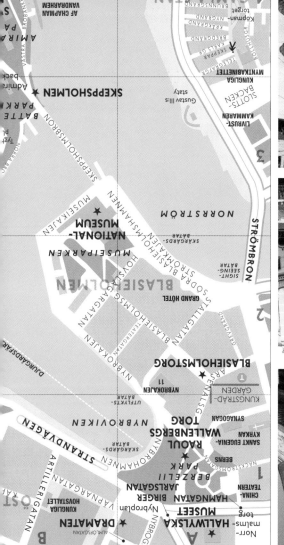

HALLWYLSKA MUSEET

DRAMATEN

B

Nybroplan / Blasieholmen / Skeppsholmen

The district around Nybroplan is the cultural heart of the city, containing several museums and the Royal Dramatic Theater, known as Dramaten. The financial complex around Blasieholmen and its famous Grand Hotel remind visitors that this is also the center of the city's money and power.

A delicate wrought-iron bridge decorated with golden crowns leads to Skeppsholmen, a royal naval base since the 17th century. Today the lush green island is home to pleasure craft, along with several museums and contemporary art galleries. It is the ideal place simply to walk and look at superb views of the old city, and marvel at the prosperous façades of Strandvägen.

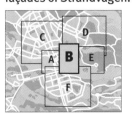

ATRIUM

VERANDAN

RESTAURANTS

Krogkonst (B B4)
→ *Amiralitetsbacken 3*
Tel. 611 99 89
Mon-Fri 11.30am–2.30pm
Grand decor and a splendid view toward Gamla stan and the Royal Palace from the outdoor terrace. Homely Swedish fare, Mediterranean food, and a great assortment of drinks (35 different beers and 40 different wines by the glass). In fine weather call ahead and order a picnic basket. 85–95 kr.

Atrium (B B3)
→ *Nationalmuseum*
Tel. 611 34 30
Tue-Sun 11am–5pm
(8pm Tue and Thu)
A light, airy space giving onto the museum's inner courtyard. Excellent vegetarian buffet and more elaborate hot dishes. 95–160 kr.

Frippe (B A1)
→ *Nybrogatan 6*
Tel. 665 61 42
Mon 11.30am–10pm;
Tue-Fri 11.30am–midnight
(1am Fri); Sat 4pm–
midnight; Sun 4–10pm
Theatergoers and actors alike bask in the atmosphere of 'artistic chic' at the restaurant of the Dramaten. Try the *Wallenbergare* (meat with

cranberries), and the wh chocolate cream desser 100–300 kr.

The Soap Bar (B A1)
→ *Nybrogatan 1*
Tel. 611 00 21
Daily 11am–3am
Office staff around here fond of this trendy mode bar beside the Dramate Great tapas (prawns, carpaccio, bruschetta et and a DJ to spin records night. 100–210 kr.

Verandan (B A2)
→ *Grand Hôtel*
Tel. 679 35 86
Daily 7am–11pm
Along with unforgettable views over the port and the Royal Palace, this is where to try the tradition Smörgåsbord, the savor Swedish buffet served i the evenings during the week, and lunchtime at weekends. Booking essential. 145–380 kr. Buffet: 395 kr.

Wedholms Fisk (B A1)
→ *Nybrokajen 17*
Tel. 611 78 74
Mon-Fri noon–11pm;
Sat 5–11pm
The place to dine on fish Wedholms Fisk has earn its popularity and presti thanks to, or despite, a nonsense, straightforwa menu. Try the boiled tur with horseradish and brown butter. 265–535 k

CARL MALMSTEN

BUKOWSKIS

CAFÉS, BARS

af Chapman (**B** B4)
→ *Flaggmansvägen 8*
Tel. 463 22 83
Mon-Sat 11am (noon Sat)–
10pm; Sat noon–10pm
A three-masted ship
converted into a youth
hostel, with a quayside
café offering enchanting
views over Gamla stan
and the Strömmen.

Pauli Café (**B** A1)
→ *Nybroplan*
Tel. 665 61 43 Mon 11.30am–
10pm; Tue-Fri 11.30am–4pm
or 7pm; Sat-Sun one hour
before the performance
The Dramaten restaurant
has a magnificent outdoor
terrace on the roof of the
theater. Eat well and
watch the boats and
vintage trams passing by.

Cadier Bar (**B** A2)
→ *Grand Hôtel; Daily 7am–*
1am (12.30am Sun-Mon)
For those who like hotel
bars the Cadier, named
after the hotel's founder,
is all elegance and
refinement. With live
piano music from 9.30pm
(Wed-Sun) and a royal
view of the castle.

V/Bar (**B** B1)
→ *Diplomat Hotel,*
Strandvägen 7 C
Mon-Fri 11.30am–midnight
(1am Thu-Fri); Sat-Sun
10pm–midnight (1am Sat)

Another hotel bar. Here
we like sitting by the
panoramic window in the
late afternoon with a glass
of champagne (interesting
prices before 7pm).

Berns Salonger B A1)
→ *Berns Hotel, Berzelii*
Park 9; Tel. 566 325015
Daily 7.30am–midnight;
brunch until 3pm Sat-Sun
When tradition meets
trend. The unfussy modern
style of British interior
designer Terence Conran is
set against the gilded
abundance of the Berns
Salonger, a magnificent
late 19th-century hall.
Here you have a choice
between brasserie- and
Asian-type food (Bistro
Bern or Berns Asian); or
just a drink at the bar.

MUSIC

Nybrokajen 11 (**B** B2)
→ *Nybrokajen 11*
Tel. 407 17 00; www.nybro
kajen11.rikskonserter.se
Founded in 1878 by
Oscar II, the former
Academy of Music
launched the careers of
such internationally
famous singers as Jussi
Björling and Birgit Nilsson.
Today the great hall is a
venue for music of all
kinds, from popular
songs to jazz.

SHOPPING

Svenskt Tenn (**B** B1)
→ *Strandvägen 5*
Tel. 670 16 00
Mon-Sat 10am–6pm (5pm
Sat); Sun noon–4pm
This interior design store
has become the symbol
of Swedish modern style.
It was founded in 1924 by
the jewelry-maker Estrid
Ericson, who later worked
with the Viennese
functionalist architect
and designer Josef Frank.
Together they created an
interior ideal where bold
designs and colors co-
existed with simple lines
and elaborate detail.

Carl Malmsten (**B** B1)
→ *Strandvägen 5 B*
Tel. 23 33 80 Mon-Sat
10am–6pm (4pm Sat)
Malmsten (1888–1972) is
one of Sweden's best-
known furniture designers.
His works were inspired by
the 19th-century fin-de-
siècle bourgeoisie, a soft
and cozy world far
removed from steel and
wooden functionalism.

Gamla lampor (**B** A1)
→ *Almlöfsgatan 3*
Tel. 611 90 35 Mon-Sat
11am–6pm (4pm Sat)
Incredibly cluttered shop
selling furniture and
mostly Scandinavian
lamps from the 1930s to

the 1970s. Designs by
Alvar Aalto, Arne Jacobsen
and Verner Panton.

Bukowskis (**B** A1)
→ *Arsenalsgatan 4*
Tel. 614 08 00
Mon-Fri 9am–5pm
Bukowskis was founded
in 1870 by the exiled
Polish nobleman Henryk
Bukowski who introduced
quality catalogued
auctions in Sweden. Today
it is the leading auction
house in Scandinavia,
worth a visit just to catch a
glimpse of a painting by
Anders Zorn (1860–1920) or
a piece of silver by Prince
Bernadotte (1907–2002).

Nutida
Svenskt Silver (**B** A1)
→ *Arsenalsgatan 3*
Tel. 611 67 18 Mon-Fri
11am–6pm; Sat noon–4pm
The Nordic home of the
silversmith's art.
The king himself buys
work from here.

Svensk Form (**B** C4)
→ *Holmamiralens väg 2*
Tel. 463 31 30
Wed 5–8pm; Thu-Sun
noon–5pm (4pm Sat-Sun);
www.svenskform.se
The shop of the Swedish
Society of Crafts and
Design, Svensk Form
stocks an amazing variety
of objects designed for
the home, beautiful as
well as practical.

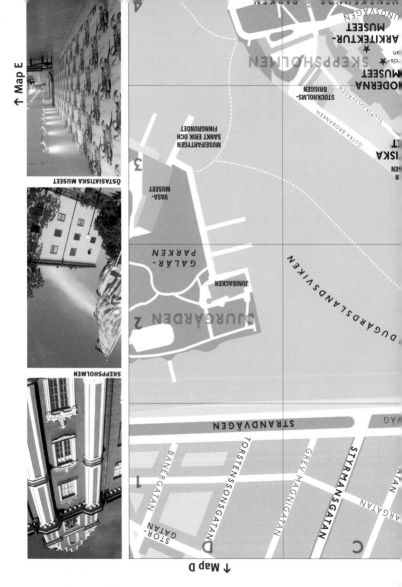

ÖSTASIATISKA MUSEET

SKEPPSHOLMEN

SKEPPSHOLMEN

ARKITEKTUR-
MUSEET

MODERNA
MUSEET

STOCKHOLMS-
BRIGGEN

SLUPSKJULSVÄGEN

ÖSTRA BROBÄNKEN

ISKA
T

MENSKINGS & PARKEN

UNDSVÄGEN

MUSEIFARTYGEN
SANKT ERIK OCH
FINNGRUNDET

VASA-
MUSEET

GALÄR-
PARKEN

JUNIBACKEN

DJURGÅRDEN 2

DJURGÅRDSBRUNNSVIKEN

STRANDVÄGEN

BANERGATAN

TORSTENSSONSGATAN

GREV MAGNIGATAN

STYRMANSGATAN

STOR-
GATAN

ARGATAN

VÄG

D

C

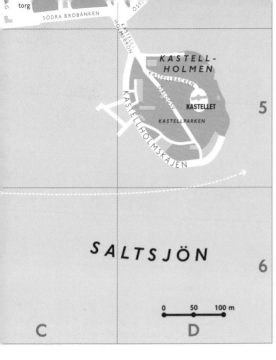

ARKITEKTURMUSEET

SVENSK FORM

mbrandt, Goya,
he entrance hall are
nous, eye-catching
(1896) by Carl
recounting the
f Swedish art and
ure .

psholmen (B B3)
the base of the
y, the 'Island of
fers a delightful
k (1 mile) around
of Stockholm.
have crossed the
Skeppsholmen,
for a fine view of
e, the cathedral,
and the heights of
the south stands
llholmen citadel,
e north the
Strandvägen

neighborhood. On the
way you can see the *af
Chapman*, the schooner
which bears the name of its
architect and builder
(1721–1808).

★ **Östasiatiska
Museet (B** B3)
→ *Tyghusplan 1*
Tel. 519 557 50
Tue-Sun 11am–5pm (8pm Tue)
Extensive collections of
Asian and Far Eastern art,
from prehistoric times to
the end of the 19th century,
with exhibits from China,
Japan, Korea and India.
This is also one of Europe's
finest collections of Chinese
pottery and porcelain
from the Song, Ming, and
Qing dynasties.

★ **Moderna Museet (B** C4)
→ *Tel. 519 552 00 Tue-Sun
10am–6pm (8pm Tue);
www.modernamuseet.se*
This rectangular temple to
20th-century art was
designed by the Spaniard
Rafael Moneo in 1995. All
the important international
figures of various art
movements (fauvists,
cubists, expressionists,
surrealists etc.) are
represented, while the
section dealing with
contemporary art has many
key works by American
artists. The superb
bookstore and self-service
cafeteria are ideally located
in front of Djurgården and
Östermalm.

★ **Arkitekturmuseet (B** C4)
→ *Tel. 587 270 14 Tue 10am–
8pm, Wed-Sun 10am–6pm*
Exhibitions on Swedish
architecture and design that
include the permanent 'Art
of building in Sweden', an
exposé of various influences
on the country's way of
living and architecture.
★ **Svensk Form (B** B4)
→ *Holmamiralens väg 2
Tel. 463 31 30
Wed 5pm–8pm; Thu-Sun
noon–5pm (4pm Sat-Sun);
www.svenskform.se*
An avant-garde gallery
backed by the Swedish
Society of Crafts and Design
shows work by young artists
and winners of the Svensk
Form Design Prize.

KUNGSHOLMENS GYMNASIUM
Jaktvarvs- plan
PONTONJÄR-PARKEN
HANTVERKARGATAN
SCHEE
PIPERSG.
KUNGSKLIPPAN
Kungsholms kyrkoplan
Bolinders plan
POLHEMSGATAN
JOHN ERICSSONS GATAN
PONTONJÄRGATAN
PIL GATAN
SÖDRA AGNEG
LÄNSSTYRELSEN
LANDSTINGS-HUSET
Kungs-holms torg
GARVARGATAN
KUNGSHOLMS KYRKA
KUNGSHOLMS HAMNPL.
PARMMÄTARGATAN
KUNGSHOLMS
SERAFENS SJUKHEM
EIRASKOLAN
SCHELIG GRÄND
SAMUEL OWENS GATA
Ragnar Östbergs plan
NORR MÄLARSTRAND
GARVA & LINDHGE
JAKOB WESTIN G.
NORR MÄLARSTRAND
STADSHU

4

RIDDARFJÄRDEN

0   150   300 m

A   B   C

CENTRALBADET

STRINDBERGSMUSEET

★ **Stadshuset** (C C4)
→ *City Hall guided tours (45 mins): Oct-May 10am, noon; June-Aug 10am, 11am, 2pm, 3pm; Sep 10am, noon, 2pm; Tower: May-Sep daily 9am–5pm*
Stockholm's most famous landmark, the city hall was built in neo-Romantic style. It took the architect Ragnar Östberg 33 years (1890–1923) to finish the building – but obvious care has been given to details both inside and out, architecturally and artistically. The Nobel banquet takes place in the brick-red Blå Hallen each year. Climb the 320-foot high tower for the best views of the city.

★ **Kungsträdgården** (C E3)
A royal garden since the Middle Ages where, well into the 17th century, fruit and vegetables were grown and harvested for the royal household. In the 18th century the King's Garden was relaid in French baroque style and opened to the public after the death of Gustav III in 1792. It is today a popular meeting place for its cafés, free concerts in summer and its ice-rink in winter. At the southern end stands the statue of Karl XII next to the Wetterling Gallery, a temple of contemporary art, containing mostly works by Anglo-Saxon artists.

★ **Sergels torg / Kulturhuset** (C D3)
The massive roundabout dedicated to Sergel (1740–1814) has, since the 1950s, been at the heart of a lively debate about urban planning. In the middle of the roaring traffic stands a glass obelisk (120 ft), known as Pinnen ('the stick'). Surrounding the square are five skyscrapers and below it lies a vast underground shopping mall. But most important of all is the City's arts center (Kulturhuset), an enormous glass and concrete structure containing exhibition spaces, theaters, a concert-hall, libraries and cafés.

★ **Konserthuset** (
→ *Hötorget 8*
Tel. 50 66 77 88 (box o
www.konserthuset.se
Ivar Tengbom (1878–
designed this conce
which was finished
with a Greek temple
The four marble sta
the main hall and th
brunnen sculpture b
steps up to the entr
by Carl Milles. On De
10 each year Konser
is the venue for the
prize-giving ceremo

★ **Olof Palmes Dödsplats** (C D2)
→ *Northeast corner of
Sveavägen and Tunne*
This is the spot whe
Palme, the former S

C

KUNGSHOLMEN

KRONOBERGS-
PARKEN

KUNGSBRON

ARLANDA
EXPRESS
FLYG- OC

BLE

KRONOBERGSG.

PARKGATAN

FLEMINGGATAN

CELSIUSG.

HANTVERKARGATAN

TEKNISKA NÄMNDHUSET

STOCKHOLMS
TINGSRÄTT

PIPERSG.

BARNHUSBRON

CARL GUSTAF
LINDSTEDTS

ÖGONSJUKHUS

SANKT
ERIKS
KAPELL

SANKT
ERIKS
GYMNASIUM

VÄSTERMALMSGALLERIAN

NEDALSGATAN

FRIDHEMS-
PLAN

SANKT ERIKSBRON

KLARASTRANDSLEDEN

Norra
Bantorget

NOR
GONF
BATHUS

KLARASTRANDSLEDEN

BARNHUSVIKEN

TORSGATAN

KUNGSHOLMS STRAND

SANKT ERIKSGATAN

ATLASGATAN

NORRBACKAG.

KAMMAKAR

WALL

STOCKHOLM
VATTEN

TEGNÉRLUNDEN

S:T PETERS-
KYRKAN

ADOLF FREDRIKS
MUSIKKLASSER

TECKENBORG

RÅDMANSGATAN

SABBATSBERGS
SJUKHUS

STOCKHOLMS
LÄNS MUSEUM

BRÅVALLAG.

FILADELFIA-
KYRKAN

STR

KUNGSTENS

TEKNOLOG

NORTULLSG.

UPPLANDSGATAN

VÄST. MANNAG.

OBSERVATORIELUND

SABBATSBERGS SJUK-
OCH ALDERDOMSHEM

VASAPARKEN

Sankt
Eriksplan

SANKT
ERIKSPLAN

BIRKA-
GATAN

RÖRSTRANDSG.

VIKINGAGATAN

TORSGATAN

TOMTEBOG

OBSERVATE
LUNDE
MUSEE

NORTULLSG.

VEGAGATAN

DALAGATAN

EASTMAN
INSTITUTET

ODENGATAN

GÄSTRIKE-
GATAN

SIGTUNA-
GATAN

BIRKA-
GATAN

INTERNAT.
BIBL.
RÅD

Spel-
bomskans
Torg

SURBRUNNSGATAN

Odenplan

JUDISKA
MUSEET

GUSTAF VASA
KYRKA

VASA KOMVUX

VASA REAL

VASASTANS
MONTESSORI
SKOLA

GUSTAF VASA
SKOLA

HÄLSINGEGATAN

FREJGATAN

KARLBERGSVÄGEN

ODENPLAN

VIDAR-
GATAN

OD

VASASTAN

KADETTIG

TEMPEL
TRÄRIAPEN

STADSHUSET

KUNGSTRÄDGÅRDEN

SERGELS TORG / KULTUR

The changes that took place during the 1950s dotted the City with American-style skyscrapers, roundabouts, and cars were given precedence over pedestrians, who were banished underground. With Sergels torg, Kulturhuset and the tower blocks around Hötorget, Stockholm received a number of new architectural landmarks. Today the City abounds with shopping malls, boutiques and restaurants. Norrmalm and Kungsholmen, on the other hand, are mainly residential neighborhoods, with quite a few houses dating from the end of the 19th and the beginning of the 20th centuries. Here the tempo is less hectic, and the restaurants and pubs have a more local character.

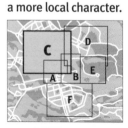

MÄLARPAVILJONGEN

BAKFICKAN

RESTAURANTS

Mälarpaviljongen (C A4)
→ *Norr Mälarstrand 64*
April-Sep: daily 11am–1am
A seasonal restaurant at the water's edge, friendly and popular with the gay community, serving a variety of light meals (mackor, herring, salads etc.) on its sunny terrace. An idyllic spot; DJ (Sat) in summer. 65–180 kr.

Bakfickan (C E3)
→ *Jakobs torg 10; Mon-Sat 11.30am (noon Sat)–11.30pm*
For excellent home-cooking in a snug, informal and dimly lit canteen: fillets of Baltic herring, salmon, sole and much more. Popular, and you'll soon see why.
100–255 kr.

Rolfs kök (C D1)
→ *Tegnérgatan 41*
Tel. 10 16 96
Mon-Fri 11.30am–1am; Sat 5pm–1am; Sun 5–11pm
Modern Swedish cuisine with Spanish and French influences. Try the ox cheek with Gotland truffles or the lingonberry-glazed reindeer fillet. Quirky, colorful decor.
155–305 kr.

Prinsen (C E3)
→ *Mäster Samuelsgatan 4*
Tel. 611 13 31
Mon-Fri 11.30am–10.30pm;
Sat 1pm–11pm; Sun 5–10pm
A favorite haunt of Stockholm's high society Prinsen probably looks exactly the same as it did in Strindberg's day. Don't miss the grilled meat and scampi salad for which the place is renowned.
169–289 kr.

East (C E2)
→ *Stureplan 13; Tel. 611 49*
Mon-Fri 11.30am–1am;
Sat-Sun 5pm–1am (3am ba
Spring rolls, Korean pancakes and tofu all feature at this hip restaurant in Stureplan. Soul and RnB in the bar (the terrace is packed in summer). 180–280 kr.

Bergamott (C B3)
→ *Hantverkargatan 35*
Tel. 650 30 34 Mon 11.30am
2pm; Tue-Fri 11.30am–2pm.
Sat 6pm–midnight
A small local restaurant in Kungsholmen that makes perfect spot for lunch, serving country salads, succulent braised tuna, steak with Roquefort and many other delights.
185–275 kr.

Kungsholmen (C B4)
→ *Norr Mälarstrand, Kajpla*
464; Tel. 505 244 50 Mon-Se
5pm–midnight (2am Thu-
Sat); Sun 3–10pm
One of the newest design restaurants of the F12 group of restaurateurs, w

E BAR

NALEN

YLLET

e dedicated to exploring
ew Swedish cuisine.
sion food that
ptivates the eye as well
the taste buds, in a
vely waterside setting.
so–325 kr.

adshuskällaren (C C4)
→ Hantverkargatan 1
. 506 322 00 Mon-Fri
30am–11pm (midnight
); Sat 5pm–midnight
luxury restaurant in the
y hall, where you can
mple what is served to
e Nobel laureates after
ey have collected their
izes. 200–400 kr;
bel Menu 1,395 kr.

ARS, CLUBS

urehof (C E2)
Stureplan 2
n-Fri 11am–2am; Sat
on–2am; Sun 5pm–2am
n't miss this classic
ench-style brasserie,
cked at weekends, or
e equally popular late-
ght bar upstairs, the O-
ren. One of the best
nues in Stureplan.

solut Ice Bar (C C3)
Nordic Sea Hotel,
saplan 4; Tel. 50 56 31 24
n-Sat 3pm–midnight
-Sat 9.45pm–1am, no
oking); Sun 3–10pm
t so unique anymore
t still fun if you've never
en in such a place: the

bar is made entirely out of
ice, and kept at −5°C all
the year round. Overcoats
and furry hoods supplied.
Booking essential.
Scandic Anglais (C E2)
→ Scandic Anglais Hotel,
Humlegårdsgatan 23
Tel. 517 340 00
Daily noon–2am
A smart hotel bar where to
unwind and escape the
cold, before doing battle
with the Stureplan clubs.
Terrace on the 7th floor.
**The Spy Bar/
Laroy (C** E2)
→ Birger Jarlsgatan 20 & 21
Tel. 545 037 01/00
The Spy Bar: Wed-Sat
10pm–5am; Laroy: Wed, Fri-
Sat 10pm–3am
Two smart clubs set side
by side, each with its own
kind of music. The Spy Bar
is elegant with a crowd of
very, very beautiful women
but very expensive drinks
and a tiny dance floor;
Laroy's still expensive but
more jolly and noisy.
Nalen (C E2)
→ Regeringsgatan 74
Tel. 505 292 00
The Mecca of dance
venues also has a calendar
of live gigs, with lunchtime
shows as well.
Fasching (C C3)
→ Kungsgatan 63
Tel. 534 829 60 Mon-Thu
7pm–1am; Fri-Sat 7pm–4am

The place for big names
in contemporary jazz.
Glenn Miller Café (C E2)
→ Brunnsgatan 21 A
Tel. 10 03 22 Mon-Thu
5–8pm; Fri-Sat 5pm–2am
Pleasant local restaurant
featuring up-and-coming
jazz musicians.

SHOPPING

Norrgavel (C E2)
→ Birger Jarlsgatan 27
Tel. 545 220 50
Mon-Sat 10am–6pm (4pm
Sat); Sun noon–4pm
Furniture, china and
household linens all in
traditional Nordic styles.
**Orrefors
& KostaBoda (C** E2)
→ Birger Jarlsgatan 15
Tel. 545 040 84 Mon-Sat
10am–6pm (4pm Sat)
Glassware shop and
showroom, in a space
designed by Per
Söderberg in 2001.
Posh Living (C D2)
→ Sveavägen 41
Tel. 23 51 55
Mon-Sat 11am–6.30pm
(4pm Sat); Sun noon–3pm
Smart, classic furniture
along with innovative
Scandinavian designs.
Yllet (C C2)
→ Drottninggatan 106
Tel. 796 76 40 Daily
11am–6pm (3pm Sat-Sun)
High-quality woolen

fabrics from Gotland and
ready-to-wear garments in
silk and linen. Gorgeous
hanks of knitting wool.
Polarn O. Pyret (C E3)
→ Hamngatan 35
Tel. 411 22 47
Mon-Sat 10am–7pm (6pm
Sat); Sun 11am–5pm
Swedish fashions for
ladies and children.
**NK – Nordiska
Kompaniet (C** E3)
→ Hamngatan 18-20
Tel. 762 80 00
Mon-Sat 10am–7pm
(6pm Sat); Sun noon–5pm
Sweden's leading
department store.
Anna Holtblad (C F2)
→ Grev Turegatan 13
Tel. 545 022 20 Mon-Sat
10.30am–6.30pm (4pm Sat)
Unpretentious clothes
made by a pioneering
Swedish couturier,
including hand-knitted
garments and attractive
bright dresses.
Biblioteksgatan (C E2)
An elegant shopping street
in Norrmalm: beautiful
handbags from **Romani**
(no. 1), audacious boots
or slippers from **Don
Donna** (no. 9), and fashion
and homeware in **Urban
Outfitters** (no. 5); the latter
is in a former Art Nouveau
movie theater and the
boutique's gilded decor
alone is worth a visit.

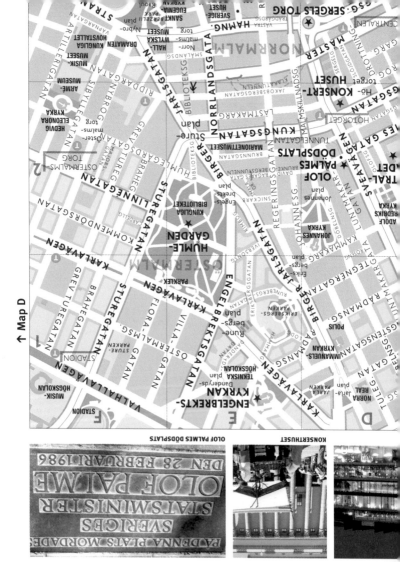

KONSERTHUSET

OLOF PALMES DÖDSPLATS

...KTSKYRKAN

HUMLEGÅRDEN

OPERAN

...nister, was
...ated on February
... as he was walking
...novie theater. This
...den's first political,
...o-be-solved, murder
...n times. Palme lies
... the nearby Adolf
...emetery.

...albadet (C D2)
...ngatan 88
...3 00
...am–8pm; Sat–Sun
...n (5pm Sun);
...albadet.se
...hese sumptuous
...eau baths (1904),
...l by the architect
...Klemming, offers
...gettable
...ce. The admission
...e time of writing:

120 kr; 170 kr at the
weekend) includes access
to the jacuzzi-bars, gym,
saunas and, best of all, the
magnificent colonnaded
swimming pool.

★ Strindbergsmuseet (C C2)
→ Drottninggatan 85
Tel. 411 53 54 Tue–Sun noon–
4pm (7pm Tue except winter);
www.strindbergsmuseet.se
August Strindberg (1849–
1912) lived here from 1908
until his death. The dining
room walls display works
by his favorite artists, the
study has kept pens and
ink bottles resting on the
desk but also Strindberg's
library, with more than
3,000 books.

★ Engelbrektskyrkan (C E1)
→ Östermalmsgatan 20
Tel. 406 98 00
Tue–Sun 11am–3pm
This Art Nouveau, neo-
Romantic church, finished
in 1914 was designed by
Lars Israel Wahlman. The
spartan interior gets most
of its unique atmosphere
from the space and height
– it is the tallest church in
Scandinavia.

★ Humlegården (C E2)
The name derives from
a thirsty Gustavus II
Adolphus, who, allegedly,
decided to plant hops
(humle) there in 1619 for
beer-making. The royal
garden with its plantations

opened to the public in
the 19th century. The
Royal Library was opened
in 1877, and the statue of
Carl Linneus, the father
of modern botany, was
unveiled in 1885. Today
Humlegården is the favorite
green space and picnic
place of many Stockholmers.

★ Operan (C E3)
→ Gustav Adolfs torg
Tel. 791 44 00
Guided tour: Sat 1pm (in
English); www.operan.se
Stockholm's opera house
was built in 1898, modeled
on the one in Paris. Its
wonderful baroque interior
is enhanced by Carl
Larsson's murals in
the foyer.

MUSIKMUSEET
ELIM KYRKAN
MUSEET
SKE
GRE
ORGATAN
OSCARS KYRKA
INNEGAT
DRAMATEN
KUNGLIGA HOVSTALLET
RIDDARGATAN
STYRMANSG
GREV
MAGNIGATAN
TORSTENSSONS
BANERGATAN
NARVAVÄGEN
FREDRIKS
HOVSLAG MUSIKAG
STORG.
VÄPNARGATAN
KAPTENSGATAN
STRANDVÄGEN
SKÄRGÅRDS-BÅTAR
NYBRO-VIKEN
MUSEISPÅRVÄG
STRANDVÄGEN
DJURGÅRDS
BRON
N
NYBROKAJEN
LADUGÅRDSLANDSVIKEN
JUNIBACKEN
Lejon-slätten
NORDISKA MUSEET
GALÄRVARV
TEATERG
HOVTULLGATAN
BLASIE-HOLMEN
MUSEIPARKEN
GALÄR-PARKEN
DJURGÅRDSV
K

A **B** **C**

SJÖHISTORISKA MUSEET

TEKNISKA MUSEET

ETN

★ **Armémuseum** (**D** A3)
→ *Riddargatan 13*
Tel. 519 563 00
Tue-Sun 11am–5pm (8pm Tue)
From Viking raids to post-World War 2 combat, the Army Museum displays over 1,000 years of fighting in a realistic series of tableaux (models, videos etc), together with exhibitions of weapons of all kinds and other militaria.

★ **Musikmuseet** (**D** A3)
→ *Sibyllegatan 2*
Tel. 519 554 90 Tue-Sun 10am–5pm (noon–5pm in winter)
The former royal bakery (1640) is now the Museum of Music, displaying instruments ancient and

modern – harp, theremin, lyre, percussion of all kinds, many of which you can try out. There is also a section devoted to music in Sweden from 1600 right up to Abba. To add to the fun, the basement has musical games to play.

★ **Strandvägen** (**D** B4)
Planned and built between 1880 and 1910, grandiose stone buildings replaced the original mishmash of wooden houses and small gardens that extended along the quayside. When Stockholm hosted the World Exhibition in 1897 Strandvägen served as a promenade to the exhibition

area in Djurgården. It is still the capital's most exclusive avenue.

★ **Historiska museet** (**D** B3)
→ *Narvavägen 13-17*
Tel. 519 556 00 Daily 11am (10am May-Sep)–5pm (8pm Thu); www.historiska.se
The National Museum of Antiquities tells the history of Sweden from prehistory to the reign of Gustav Vasa (10000 BC–16th century) including the Vikings (c.800–1050); with a fabulous skeleton about 8,750 years old, an elk's head carved out of diorite, jewels and superb medieval wooden sculptures. The

dazzling Gold Roor underground vault with gold and silve dating from 2000– and look out for an astonishing collar with 458 figures.

★ **Diplomatstade**
The diplomatic qua paradise for jogger peaceful place to s beside the water, c Djurgården. Furthe are groups of gran with prettily colore façades. Look out attractive Anglican Engelska kyrkan (1

★ **Sjöhistoriska museet** (**D** F4)
→ *Djurgårdsbrunns*

D

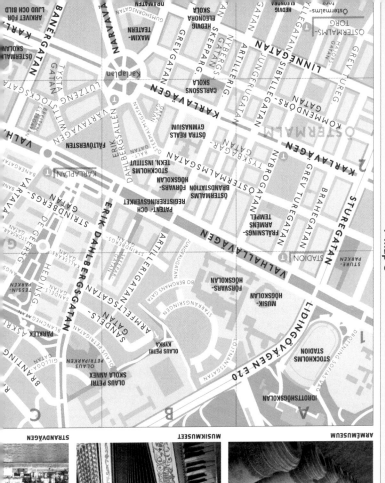

ARMÉMUSEUM

MUSIKMUSEET

STRANDVÄGEN

Östermalm

Far from Stockholm's medieval center, the district of Östermalm was developed much later. Until 1885 it was known as Ladugårdslandet ('farms land'), and was mainly property of the Crown. In the 1870s Stockholm underwent a period of expansion, and the neighborhood began to change. Modeled on Paris, it developed elegant houses, star-shaped squares, avenues and boulevards. Wealthy citizens were the first to move in, and still live here today. Östermalm has grand apartments, fine restaurants, exclusive shops, art galleries and several big museums, but its proximity to the large green space of Gärdet and Djurgården's oak woods makes it a haven of peace.

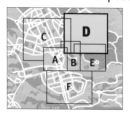

ERIKS BAKFICKA

AUBERGINE

RESTAURANTS

Örtagården (**D** A3)
→ Nybrogatan 31
Tel. 662 17 28
Mon-Fri 10am–11pm (buffet 10am–2pm); Sat-Sun 11am–11pm (no buffet)
The lavish vegetarian buffet is the star attraction of this restaurant, situated above Östermalm market. Piano music in the background. Meat and fish dishes in the room next door. 85 kr for lunch, 135 kr for dinner.

Brasserie Godot (**D** A3)
→ Grev Turegatan 36
Tel. 660 06 14
Mon-Sat 5pm–1am
You may wait in vain for the elusive Godot, but there's no shortage of celebrities in this smart bistro, which serves classic French dishes enlivened by some rustic local touches and the chef's creative flair. Terrace in summer. Bar and excellent wine list. 115–225 kr.

Elverket (**D** B3)
→ Linnég. 69
Tel. 661 25 62 Mon 11am–2pm; Tue-Fri 11am–2pm, 5–11pm; Sat 5–11pm
A restaurant, bar and theater. The first, trendy and cool, offers flavorsome daily changing

dishes: roast lamb, turbo mousse, artichoke and rocket salad. Finish off w a combo: one scoop of i cream, one espresso an one calvados. 125–270 k

Eriks Bakficka (**D** C4)
→ Fredrikshovsgatan 4
Tel. 660 15 99 Mon-Fri 11.30am–midnight (11pm Mon), Sat 5pm–midnight
A blackboard announces the kvällens husmans (dis of the day) in this elegar restaurant. Don't miss th shellfish casserole, the Biff Rydberg (diced sirlo with onions and egg) or pyttipanna. 120–295 kr.

Aubergine (**D** B2)
→ Linnég. 38
Tel. 660 02 04 Mon-Fri 11.30am–midnight (1am Fr Sat 5pm–1am
A team of four young che have transformed this lo eating-house into a sma restaurant at affordable prices. The cooking is Franco-Italian, and the ambience elegant. Diner can also eat at the bar, where the prices are low 175–265 kr.

Villa Källhagen (**D** E3)
→ Djurgårdsbrunnsv. 10
Tel. 665 03 10
Mon-Sat 11.30am–10pm; Sun 11.30am–5pm
Grilled arctic char on a b of fennel and asparagus with horseradish sauce i

NORDISKA GALLERIET

ÖSTERMALMS SALUHALL

one of the specialties of this traditional restaurant. At lunchtime choose to eat outside on the terrace with views over the bay of Djurgårdsbrunn, and perhaps for the lighter, more simple bistro menu. 35–345 kr.

Paul & Norbert (D A4**)**
→ Strandvägen 9
Tel. 663 81 83 Mon 6–11pm; Tue-Fri noon–2pm, 6–11pm; Sat 6–11pm
Small, discreet and incredibly sophisticated restaurant. Master chef Norbert Lang's exquisite seasonal cuisine – French with a Swedish twist – has earned him cult status among his colleagues throughout Scandinavia. Try grouse, elk, reindeer and other wild flavors from the North. 195 kr at lunch; set menus 800–1,000 kr.

CAFÉS, BARS

Foam (D B2**)**
→ Karlav. 75
Mon-Fri 10am–9pm; Sat-Sun 11am–7pm
So keen on design even the menu mentions furniture. A very special place and the sandwiches are delicious.

Oscars (D C3**)**
→ Narvavägen 32
Tel. 662 52 26

Mon-Fri 8am–7pm; Sat-Sun 10am–6.30pm
A large selection of teas, mackor, hot dish of the day, gigantic, wholesome healthy salads and delicious brownies.

Strandbryggan (D C4**)**
→ Strandvägen 27
Tel. 660 37 14
Daily 11am–1am
Right by the water near Djurgård Bridge. Canoes on hire for those looking for a bit more excitement.

Skafferiet (D D3**)**
→ Radiohuset, Oxenstiernsgatan 20
Mon-Fri 8am–5pm (4pm Fri)
Undervalued hang-out for media spies, atop the Kaknästornet, with panoramic view over Stockholm.

Tudor Arms (D B3**)**
→ Grevg. 31
Mon-Fri 11.30am–11pm; Sat 1–11pm; Sun 1–7pm
Stockholm's first pub (1969). Draft beer and sandwiches.

Nox (D A3**)**
→ Grev Turegatan 30
Tel. 545 82 400
Tue-Thu 5pm–1am; Fri 4pm–1am; Sat 6pm–1am
Before heading off to the clubs, relax with a cocktail in the pleasant summer garden of this trendy bar-restaurant. DJ on Friday and Saturday nights.

SHOPPING

The area around Nybrogatan is home to many antique dealers and designers.

Nordiska Galleriet (D A3**)**
→ Nybrogatan 11
Tel. 442 83 60 Mon-Sat 10am–6pm; Sun noon–4pm
The gallery has been selling furniture and other pieces by famous Swedish and European designers since 1913 – Arne Jacobsen, Mackintosh, Philippe Starck. The wide variety of articles, many in brilliant colors, arranged on two floors is a fascinating sight.

Asplund (D A3**)**
→ Sibyllegatan 31
Tel. 662 52 84 Mon-Sat 11am–6pm (4pm Sat)
Again, work by the best Swedish designers (Jonas Bohlin, Thomas Sandell, Pia Wallén), together with international names (Tom Dixon, Piero Lissoni , Marc Newson), chosen by the Asplund brothers.

Wahlström, Tropius Antik (D A2**)**
→ Nybrogatan 42
Tel. 662 33 37
Mon-Fri noon–6pm (and Sat noon–3pm in Sep-April)
Late 18th- and early 19th-century furniture and

objets d'art, including pieces from Russia.

Östermalms Saluhall (D A3**)**
→ Östermalmstorg
Mon-Sat 9.30am–6pm (6.30pm Fri; 4pm Sat)
Stockholm's best indoor market, with a slate-clad bell tower, built in 1889. There is a good Swedish canteen here called Nybroe, with fish and seafood available at Lisa Elmqvist and Gerdas.

Svensk Slöjd (D A3**)**
→ Nybrog. 23
Tel. 663 66 50 Mon-Sat 11am–6pm (3pm Sat)
A souvenir shop selling the ubiquitous dalahästar (wooden horses from the Dalarna region), but also a selection of textiles and wooden objects from all over Sweden.

Indiska (D A3**)**
→ Nybrog. 27
Tel. 660 20 00 Mon-Sat 10am–6.30pm (5pm Sat)
This Swedish chain store has been adding an exotic Indian touch to Swedish homes since 1901.

Jacksons (D A2**)**
→ Sibylleg. 53
Tel. 665 33 50 Mon-Fri noon–6pm; Sat 11am–3pm
Fun second-hand shop with Scandinavian, Italian and American furniture from 1880 to 1980.

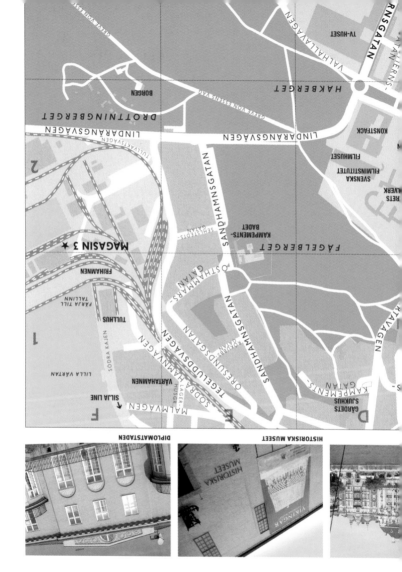

KAKNÄSTORNET

MAGASIN 3

i49 00
10am–5pm;
historiska.nu
utiful round white
g of the National
e Museum (1930)
igned by Ragnar
, who also designed
hall. Here, Sweden's
e history is
ed through ships,
models (cargo ships,
s, liners), paintings,
otographs.
tableware are
display.

grafiska
★ (**D** F4)
árdsbrunnsvägen 34
'50 00
10am–5pm (8pm

Wed); Sat-Sun 11am–5pm;
www.etnografiska.se
Travel beyond Europe at the
Ethnography Museum
through a multitude of
exotic objects: African
masks made of crocodile
skin, an Inuit coat made of
polar bear fur, a Mongolian
tent... The cafeteria alone
is worth a visit for its
delicious exotic food.

★ **Tekniska museet** (**D** F4)
→ Museivägen 7
Tel. 450 56 00
Mon-Fri 10am–5pm (8pm
Wed); Sat-Sun 11am–5pm;
www.tekniskamuseet.se
The history of Swedish
technology and industry,
through exhibits on mining

techniques, iron ore
production, etc. Huge
industrial hall with classic
cars from 1897, the
country's oldest steam
engine, bicycles, aircraft.
Lavish and innovative
science center, Teknorama,
where children or young
people can learn about
science and the laws of
nature through hands-on
experience, and a recent
attraction, Cino4, a four-
dimensional movie theater
where all senses are
called upon.

★ **Kaknästornet** (off **D** F3)
→ Mörka kroken 28-30
Tel. 667 21 05 Open daily;
June-Aug: 9am–10pm; Sep-

Dec: 10am–9pm (5pm Sun);
Jan-April: 10am–5pm (9pm
Thu-Sat; 6pm Sun)
The 509-foot high TV and
telegraph tower was for a
long time the tallest
building in Scandinavia.
Viewing platform on levels
30 and 31 with restaurant,
café, and stupendous views.

★ **Magasin 3** (**D** F2)
→ Frihamnen; Tel. 545 680 40
Thu-Sun noon–5pm (7m
Thu); www.magasin3.com
Sweden's largest private
art gallery, opened in 1987
in a 1930s warehouse, has
attracted the most attention
lately for its bold and
provocative exhibits of
contemporary art.

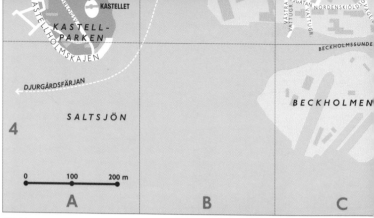

KASTELLET

KASTELL-PARKEN

KASTELLHOLMSKAJEN

DJURGÅRDSFÄRJAN

SALTSJÖN

4

0   100   200 m

A   B   C

VÄSTRA VATTUGR / UGATAN NORDENSKIÖLD / VÄGE

BECKHOLMSSUNDE

BECKHOLMEN

ASTELLHOLMSKAJEN

DJURGÅRDSSTADEN

SKANSEN

ROSENDALS SLOTT

★ **Junibacken** (**E** A1)
→ *Galärvarvsvägen*
Tel. 587 230 00 June-Aug:
daily 10am–5pm (7pm July);
Sep-May: Tue-Sun 10am–5pm;
www.junibacken.se
A fairytale museum, whose main attraction is the small train ride through a miniature Astrid Lindgren (1907–2002) world, where children meet the Swedish author's beloved characters. Children's books in several languages in the bookshop.

★ **Nordiska Museet** (**E** B1)
→ *Djurgårdsvägen 6-16*
Tel. 519 546 00
Sep-May: Mon-Fri 10am–4pm,
Sat-Sun 11am–5pm;
June-Aug: daily 10am–5pm;
www.nordiskamuseet.se

The daily life and work of the Swedish people from the 16th century to the present day portrayed in a monumental building from 1907, built in the so-called Vasa Renaissance style. The permanent exhibits cover areas like tradition, fine tableware, fashion, textiles and furniture. Temporary exhibitions too.

★ **Vasamuseet** (**E** A2)
→ *Galärvarvsvägen 14*
Tel. 519 548 00 June-Aug:
daily 8.30am–6pm; Sep-May:
daily 10am–5pm (8pm
Wed); www.vasamuseet.se
Djurgården's star attraction and a must in Stockholm. The 160-foot tall Vasa ship, with its 700 gilded wooden

sculptures and 64 bronze cannons, was meant to be the jewel in Sweden's imperial crown. But it capsized and sank shortly after its launching in 1628. It was salvaged almost intact – from the impressive figureheads to the simplest food tin – in 1961. In 1990, after an amazing restoration work, the Vasa Museum was opened, literally built around the wrecked ship which visitors can now board. No doubt it is one of the world's most original museums.

★ **Aquaria Vattenmuseum** (**E** B2)
→ *Falkenbergsgatan 2*
Tel. 660 90 89 Tue-Sun 10am–4.30pm (daily until 6pm June

15–Aug 15); www.aq
An aquarium with a reconstruction of a ladder with Baltic s rainforest and its ve frogs and a shark ta for fish-enthusiasts children.

★ **Liljevalchs** (**E** B
→ *Djurgårdsvägen 6*
Tel. 508 313 30
Tue-Sun 11am–5pm (
Tue and Thu in Sep-M
The Liljevalchs is he a magnificent neoc house (1916), and contemporary art exhibitions all year (drawings, engravin photographs, video The Spring show is annual highlight.

E

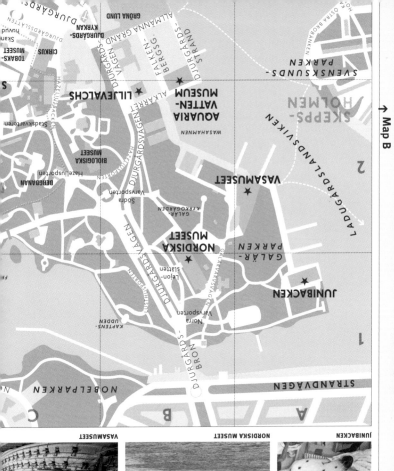

JUNIBACKEN

NORDISKA MUSEET

VASAMUSEET

Djurgården

Ever since King Karl XI turned Djurgården into a royal hunting ground in the 17th century the island has been the city's most popular green space and the Stockholmers' favorite playground – one of their Sunday rituals is a visit to Skansen open-air museum or a dizzying ride at one of Gröna Lund attractions. Don't forget to go and admire the *Vasa*, preserved intact after it sank on its maiden voyage in the 17th century. Nearby are some beautiful villas which have been turned into sumptuous art galleries. And finally get nature with a 4-mile walk around the bay of Djurgårdsbrunn, past lakes with wildfowl, and herons waiting patiently at the water's edge.

BLÅ PORTEN

ROSENDALS TRÄDGÅRDSCAFÉ

RESTAURANTS

Blå Porten (E B2)
→ Djurgårdsvägen 64
Tel. 663 87 59
Daily 11am–5pm (9pm Tue, Thu); May-Aug: daily 11am–10pm (7pm Sat-Sun)
A popular venue for art lovers and Sunday morning strollers is this little restaurant beside the Liljevalchs art gallery, serving good home-cooked food and delicious cakes. 85–125 kr.

Stora Gungan (E C3)
→ Skansen; Tel. 660 66 01
Daily 11.30am–8pm (4pm winter); open Sat-Sun only in Jan-Feb
In a pretty little cottage at Skansen is a restaurant serving good traditional food eaten either inside beside the decorated porcelain stove or out on the beautiful terrace, opposite the bell towers of Gamla stan. 85–130 kr.

Carl Michael (E B3)
→ Allmänna gränd 6
Tel. 667 45 96
Mon 11.30am–3pm; Tue-Fri 11.30am–midnight; Sat-Sun 1pm–midnight
A classy restaurant opposite Gröna Lund, decorated in cool white and beige and named after the 18th-century singer, poet and composer Carl Michael Bellman. The cooking is traditional Swedish (with a terrific blood pudding). 80–260 kr.

Lisapåudden (off E F4)
→ Biskopsvägen 7
Tel. 660 94 75
Mon 11.30am–5pm; Tue-Fri 11.30am–10pm; Sat-Sun noon–5pm
A smart, contemporary restaurant right at the water's edge beside the neighboring marina. It's a friendly place which specializes in seafood as well as traditional Swedish cuisine: try the 'Skagen toast' (with prawns and mayo), or kalixlöjron (bleak roe). 92–235 kr.

Ulla Winbladh (E C2)
→ Rosendalsvägen 8
Tel. 534 89 701
Daily 11.30am (noon Sat-Sun)–11pm
Much praised in local gastronomic circles, this restaurant opened in 1897 as a bakery for the Stockholm International Expo. Go for the gratin of stuffed Baltic herring, köttbullar à la crème, and vanilla ice cream with hjortron. There is also a reasonably priced self-service section on the terrace. 105–300 kr.

ASARESTAURANGEN

SKANSENBUTIKEN

NORDISKA MUSEET

illa Godthem (E C2)
→ Rosendalsvägen 9
el. 661 07 22
ue-Fri 11.30am–11pm
midnight Fri); Sat noon–
idnight; Sun noon–10pm
his fairytale Swiss-style
lla with a view of
jurgårdsbrunnsviken
ates from 1874. Originally
uilt for the popular singer
ddman, it became a
estaurant in 1897, and
erves interesting dishes
ke reindeer meat with
ngonberry sauce and
lderflower sorbet.
75–295 kr. Menu 245 kr.

AFÉS

**osendals
rädgårdscafé (E** E2)
→ Rosendalsterrassen 12
el. 545 812 70
lay-Sep: daily 11am–5pm
5pm Sat-Sun); Oct, Feb-
arch: Tue-Sun 11am–4pm;
pril: 11am–5pm
ery pleasant café serving
rganic food in the heart
f Djurgården. Weather
ermitting you eat under
e apple trees, otherwise
ou retreat to the tables in
e conservatory. Rhubarb
ie in season.

**asarestaurangen
E** A2)
→ Vasamuseet; Tel. 661 16 20
aily 9.30am–5.30pm
1am–4pm inSep-May)

The museum's café-
restaurant. Look out for
the 17th-century menu
with delicacies like dried
fruit marinated in rum and
served with cardamom
ice cream and skorpor
(small toasted rolls).

**Rosendals
Wärdshus (E** E2)
→ Rosendalsterrassen 3
Tel. 661 39 70
Daily 11am–10pm
Less known than its
hyped neighbor but
quieter and with a more
beautiful view. Reasonably
good food.

Café Ektorpet (E E4)
→ Waldemarsudde
June-Aug: daily 11am–5pm
An old-fashioned wooden
shed at the entrance to
Waldemarsudde, just
perfect for a relaxing snack
or a drink.

Skansen (E C2)
This open-air museum
has several cafés serving
coffee and snacks:
Café Gubbhyllan:
excellent mackor and
homemade kanelbulle;
Café Petissan: a small
konditori for ladies;
Solliden: its terrace
attracts crowds of tourists
in the summer with a
daily smörgåsbord and a
Swedish popular song
evening (allsångskvällar)
every Tuesday until 9pm.

**Flickorna Helin &
Voltaire (E** C2)
→ Rosendalsvägen 14
Tel. 664 51 08 Daily 9am–
5pm (10am–8pm summer)
Stop here for coffee and
cakes after visiting
Skansen. It's in an
impressive brick and
ceramic pavilion left over
from the International
Expo of 1897. The nött
bomber, homemade
walnut cakes, are
gorgeous and
scrumptious.

AMUSEMENT PARK

Gröna Lund (E B3)
→ April-mid-Sep: last
weekend of the month
11am–11pm (times may
vary); www.gronalund.com
The oldest amusement
park in Sweden, with the
traditional roller-coasters,
bumper cars, hall of
mirrors, raffles... Plays for
children during the day,
concerts in the evening.

SHOPPING

**Rosendals Trädgårds-
butik & Plantbod (E** F2)
→ Rosendalsterrassen 12
Tel. 545 812 70
Tue-Sun 11am–4pm
Organically grown fruit
and vegetables. Also sells
marmalade, jams,

preserves – all their own
produce, as well as herbs,
spices and design
gardening tools.

Skansenbutiken (E C3)
→ Djurgårdsslätten 49
(next to entrance to Skansen)
Tel. 442 82 68
June-Aug: daily 11am–7pm;
May, Sep: 11am–6pm;
Oct-April: 11am–5pm (4pm
Jan-Feb)
A boutique with an
unusually good selection of
designer objects, as well as
craftware from Skansen in
wood, glass and pottery.

Skansen (E C2-3)
Several boutiques
scattered through the park:
Vaktstugan (books,
souvenirs and postcards),
Kryddboden (a mid-19th-
century general store with
sweets, tea and other odds
and ends), **Krukmakeriet**
(stoneware pots),
Stockholms Glasbruk
(tableware and ornamental
glass), **Skansen-Akvariet,
Björnboden** (toys and soft
toys), **Marknadsgatan/
Bollnästorget** (souvenirs
and crafts from Skansen.

Nordiska museet (E B1)
→ www.nordiskamuseet.se
The museum shop sells
copies of objects from their
collection. The large book
department has one of
Sweden's best historical
literature sections.

↓ Map D

VATTENMUSEUM

LILJEVALCHS

DJURGÅRDS-

SINGELKROKEN

Sollids-porten

BELLMANSBYSTEN

VÄRDSHUSVÄGEN

BELLMANS VÄG

SIRISHOVSVÄGEN

Bellmanso-porten

GAHOLM

SEGLORA KYRKA

orgel

ORANGERIVÄGEN

ORANGERIET

2

ROSENDALS TERRASSEN

ROSENDALS TRÄDGÅRD

Lill-Skansen

BREDABLICK

HÖGLOFTET

DEN

Rosendals Terrass

★ ROSENDALS SLOTT

SIRISHOVSVÄGEN

SIRISHOV

BJÖRNBERGET

ROSENDALSVÄGEN

DE BESCHES VÄG

ÄLSVÄGEN

KÄRLEKS-UDDEN

1

← DJURGÅRDSBRUNN

DJURGÅRDSBRUNNSVIKEN

TEKNISKA MUSEET

SJÖHISTORISKA MUSEET

FOLKE BERNADOTTES VÄG

E

D

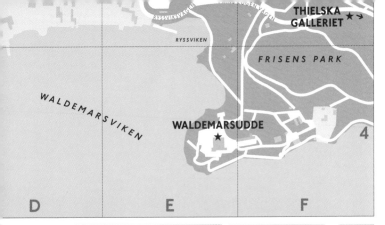

Map showing THIELSKA GALLERIET, FRISENS PARK, RYSSVIKEN, RYSSVIKSVÄGEN, WALDEMARSVIKEN, WALDEMARSUDDE, PRINS EUGENS VÄGEN

D   E   F   4

WALDEMARSUDDE

THIELSKA GALLERIET

gårdsstaden (E C3)
ctive group of small
shed cottages
om the 17th
when they were
workers in the
ckyard at
vet and the tar
at Beckholmen.

sen (E C2)
2 80 00 May-mid-
y 10am–8pm;
-Aug: 10am–10pm;
n–5pm; Oct-April:
m; www.skansen.se
d's first open-air
was opened by
azelius in 1891, with
lings from different
he country, urban
. It is designed as
useum so you can

watch the glassworks, the
joiners and the mechanics
at work. The zoo has Nordic
animals like bears, wolves,
elk, reindeer living in natural
habitats. Special events
include the performance
of folk dances in summer
and a Christmas market.

★ Rosendals slott (E F2)
→ Rosendalsvägen
Tel. 402 61 30 Open Tue-Sun
in June-Aug; guided tours:
noon, 1pm, 2pm and 3pm
Superb country house in
Empire style, and the best
example of the Swedish Karl
Johan style. The magnificent
interior has barely changed
since King Karl XIV Johan
(reigned 1818–44), for
whom the place was built,

and Queen Desirée lived
here during the 1820s.

★ Waldemarsudde (E E4)
→ Prins Eugens vägen 6
Tel. 662 47 40 Tue-Sun
11am–5pm (8pm Thu);
www.waldemarsudde.com
The large villa, built in a
mixture of Art Nouveau and
Swedish manor-house
styles, was designed in
1905 by Ferdinand Boberg
for 'the Painter Prince',
Eugene. The collection
includes the prince's own
works, his first-class
painting and sculpture
collection of Swedish art
from 1880 to 1945 (Bergh,
Johnsson, Larsson, Milles,
Zorn). Numerous temporary
exhibitions.

★ Thielska galleriet
(off E F3)
→ Sjötullsbacken 8
Tel. 662 58 84
Mon-Sat noon–4pm;
Sun 1–4pm; www.thielska-
galleriet.se
Ernest Thiel (1859–1947)
was a banker and art
collector who built a house
in 1907 and hung it with
works he purchased from
his artist friends, including
Carl Larsson, Bruno Liljefors,
Anders Zorn and the
Norwegian Edvard Munch.
The state acquired his
collection in 1924 and
opened it to the public in
this splendid villa designed
by Ferdinand Boberg
(1860–1946).

KATARINA KYRKA

FJÄLLGATAN

KÅKAR

★ **Stadsmuseet** (**F** B1)
→ Ryssgården, Slussen
Tel. 508 31 620
Tue-Sun 11am–5pm (8pm
Thu); www.stadsmuseum.
stockholm.se
Housed in a baroque
building (1685) built by
Tessin the Elder, the City
Museum traces the
evolution of the city and the
life of its inhabitants from
prehistoric times to
the present day. There are
archeological remains, and
reconstructions of various
places such as an 18th-
century cellar, a worker's
lodging in the 19th century
and an elementary school
from the early 20th century.
Look out too for temporary

exhibitions on
contemporary themes.
★ **Katarinahissen** (**F** C1)
→ Mid-May-Aug:
daily 8am–10pm;
Sep-mid-May: 10am–6pm
This original elevator was
driven by steam from its
opening in 1883 until the
mid-1910s when it switched
to electricity. It was then
replaced by a more modern
version. Take the giddy-
making 124-foot ride to
magnificent views over
the old part of the city,
Mosebacke and the sea.
★ **Almgrens
sidenväveri** (**F** B1)
→ Repslagargatan 15A
Tel. 642 56 16
Mon-Fri 10am–4pm; Sat-Sun

11am–3pm; www.kasiden.se
A beautifully preserved
silk-weaving mill which
opened in 1883, and where
for generations the Almgren
family have been producing
finest quality fabric in the
traditional fashion using
original Jacquard patterns.
Here too you can see the
workers at their looms,
along with displays of silk
specially woven for the
royal family.
★ **Bofills båge /
Söder torn** (**F** B2)
→ Medborgarplatsen
The residential curved
building (båge means
'bow') of the Spanish
architect Ricardo Bofill and
the tower of the Danish

architect Henning [...]
caused a great stir [...]
they were built in th[...]
Many people cons[...]
the buildings too b[...]
severe, too unSwe[...]
too close to the Lili[...]
huset, a 17th-centu[...]
mansion on the no[...]
corner of the squar[...]
often, many others[...]
these unconventio[...]
constructions were[...]
welcome addition t[...]
already colorful Sö[...]
district. See what y[...]
★ **Moskén** (**F** C2)
→ Kapellgränd 10
Tel. 509 109 00 Mon[...]
5pm; Sat-Sun noon–[...]
Originally a power [...]
designed in 1903 b[...]

F

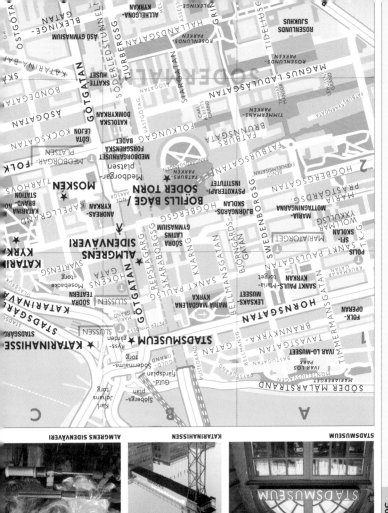

ALMGRENS SIDENVÄVERI

KATARINAHISSEN

STADSMUSEUM

↓ Ma

↓ Map A

The southern suburb of Södermalm has become the capital's hippest island ever since it was colonized by a crowd of eccentric, laid-back writers, artists and media folk who loved this former working-class district. South of Folkungagatan, the alternative quarter of SoFo is filled with cafés, junk shops, exotic restaurants, designer and fashion boutiques, and smart antique dealers. 'Söder' jealously guards its freedom and its unorthodox lifestyle. It's no accident that the district has its own mosque, while its famous theater, the Södra Teatern, stages many multicultural shows.

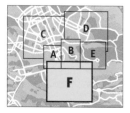

CAFÉ BLÅ LOTUS

EN FUL OCH EN GUL

RESTAURANTS

Café Blå Lotus (F C3)
→ *Katarina bangata 21*
Mon-Fri 2am–8pm (7pm Fri);
Sat-Sun 10am–7pm
A predominantly feminine clientèle have lost their hearts to this peaceful café-restaurant with its lively ethnic decor. Varied menu. 30–65 kr.

Chutney (F C3)
→ *Katarina bangata 19*
Daily 11am (noon Sat-Sun)–10pm
A little vegetarian basement restaurant in SoFo where low prices and generous helpings are the rule. Friendly welcome and world music, with an outside terrace in summer. 70–140 kr.

Snotty (F D2)
→ *Skånegatan 90*
Daily 4pm–1am
Köttbullar with risotto: no-frills cooking in this tiny bar-restaurant decorated with album sleeves, where the cocktails are named after rock bands. It's an informal, hospitable place playing good music; DJ (Wed-Sat). 90–200 kr.

Pelikan (F C3)
→ *Blekingegatan 40*
Tel. 556 090 90
Mon-Fri 3.30pm–1am;
Sat-Sun 1pm–1am

This old Swedish beer ha specializes in quality home-cooking: mashed turnips with boiled pickl pork, fried bacon with onion sauce, pittypanna and the typical Baltic herrings. 123–189 kr.

Back A Yard (F D2)
→ *Folkungagatan 128*
Tel. 644 94 94
Wed-Sun 6–11pm
A bit of Old Jamaica in th heart of Stockholm, with great ethnic dishes such jerk chicken or curry goa with *ackee*, and reggae playing in the backgrour Irresistible! 130–215 kr.

Koh Phangan (F C2)
→ *Skånegatan 57*
Tel. 642 68 65 Mon-Fri 110 1am; Sat-Sun 2pm–1am
Colored lamps and bamb for an exotic atmosphere and a lot of lime and swe chilli sauce in the dishes Try *Tom Kha Gai*, a chicke soup with coconut milk a fresh coriander, or the Th green curry with shrimps 135–265 kr.

En ful och en gul (F E2
→ *Erstagatan 22*
Tel. 643 71 80 Tue-Fri 5–9p Sat-Sun 4–10pm
Skillets sizzle and pots simmer merrily while flames flicker in the wok but the dining-room remains a haven of calm The Asiatic food here is

AL

TIOGRUPPEN

KONSTHANTVERKARNA

...o be bettered: just
sample the *Chou Ya Zi*
grilled duck) or their Hong
Kong Soup. 176–246 kr.

CAFÉS, BARS

String Café (**F** D2)
→ Nytorgsgatan 38
Tel. 714 85 14
Mon-Fri 9.30am–9pm,
Sat-Sun 10.30am–7pm
Chairs that don't match,
and a checkerboard floor:
this is bohemian life in
SoFo with a vengeance,
and the young arty set
who come here wouldn't
change a thing.
Gondolen (**F** C1)
→ Katarinahissen
Tel. 641 70 90 Mon-Fri
noon–1am; Sat 4pm–1am
Sitting high above sea
level, you'd think you were
in an airborne Orient
Express with the most
amazing views of Lake
Mälaren and the Baltic –
very romantic. Try the
cocktail Hemingway.
Mosebacke (**F** C1)
→ Mosebacke torg 3
Tel. 556 098 90 Mon-Fri
1pm–1am (2am Fri), Sat-Sun
0.30am–2am (1am Sun)
The unmissable venue
for alternative culture in
Södermalm. Different
rooms for different styles
of music (rock, jazz,
reggae), and a terrace

famous for its views over
the city. Concerts in the
evening (Sep–May).
Sjögräs (**F** A1)
→ Timmermansgatan 24
Tel. 84 12 00
Mon-Sat 6pm–1am
Upstairs is a trendy bar
and restaurant, while in
the basement you can
sip the finest rums in
Stockholm while listening
to the techno sounds that
DJs spin every night.
Café Rival (**F** A1)
→ Hotel Rival,
Mariatorget 3; Tel. 545 78900
Mon-Fri 8am– 8pm; Sat-Sun
9am–7pm
The brightly colored café
of the sleek Art Deco hotel.
Very good patisserie and
bread from the Rival
Bakery next door.
**Debaser Slussen/
Debaser Medis** (**F** B1-2)
→ Karl Johanstorg 1
and Medborgarplatsen 8
Tel. 462 98 60
Two very popular venues
for pop and rock concerts.

SHOPPING

Götgatan (**F** B1)
Tiogruppen (no. 25)
→ www.tiogruppen.com
Group of ten, now cult,
Swedish textile designers.
Bold colors and patterns.
c/o Stockholm (no. 30)
→ www.costockholm.se

Two floors of trendy
clothing.
Bruno
Götgatsbacken (no. 36)
Cool designer shopping
mall with a glass-covered
central courtyard,
Ljunggrens, that is both
a coffee shop and a
lounge. The 'concept
store' at its best.
Designtorget (no. 51)
→ www.designtorget.se
Clever objects and plenty
of designer gadgets.
Coctail (**F** D2)
→ Bondeg. 34 / Skåneg. 71
Tel. 642 07 40 Mon-Fri
noon–6pm, Sat-Sun 11am
(noon Sun)–4pm
Kitsch Coctail stocks odds
and ends from around the
world.
Tjallamalla (**F** D2)
→ Bondeg. 46
Tel. 640 78 47 Daily noon–
6pm (4pm Sat; 3pm Sun)
250 young designers are
represented in this little
temple to the goddess of
fashion.
Pet Sounds (**F** C2)
→ Skåneg. 53
Tel. 702 97 98
Mon-Sat 11am–7pm (5pm
Sat); Sun 1–5pm
A legendary record store
that now also sells books.
Across the street is the
sister Pet Sounds Bar, a
glamorous and fun bar-
restaurant.

Bric-a-brac (**F** A2)
→ Swedenborgsgatan 5A
Tel. 643 75 00
Mon-Sat 11am–6pm (4pm
Sat); Sun noon–4pm
Sober, minimalist men's
and women's fashion with
a touch of the Far East.

GALLERIES

Konsthantverkarna
(**F** B1)
→ Södermalmstorg 4
Mon-Sat 11am–6pm (4pm Sat)
Excellent selection of
objets (glass, metal, wood,
ceramics) in the city's
oldest co-operative.
Hornsgatspuckeln (**F** A1)
→ Hornsgatan 2-50
Up to Mariatorget the street
is full of art galleries and
arts & crafts shops:
ceramics and glass at Blås
& Knåda (no. 26,
www.blasknada.com),
contemporary paintings at
Södra Galleriet (no. 34),
decorative objects and
original silver jewellery at
Smide och Form (no. 36),
and innovative
Scandinavian ceramics at
Kaolin (no. 50).
125 kvadrat (**F** C2)
→ Kocksgatan 17
Tel. 640 97 77 Daily 11am–
6pm (4pm Sat-Sun)
Co-operative selling glass,
silver, textiles, pottery and
wooden products.

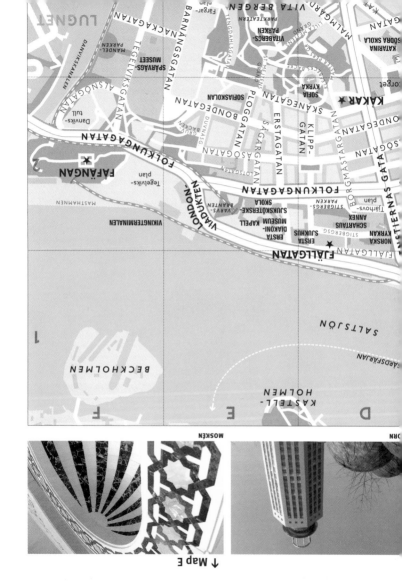

↓ Map E

KOLONIOMRÅDEN

architect of its day,
d Boberg. His
influences and the
ian-Moroccan style
ilding came in
hen the building
verted into a
in 2000. The
ngine room can
 people.

rina kyrka (F C2**)**
rgsgatan 13
800 Mon–Fri 11am–
-Sun 10am–5pm
 kyrka was the first
holm's three dome-
churches to be
d was finished in
ng Karl X Gustav,
 to build a new
 the nearby
ke torg, insisted

on building an imposing
church, making it a puzzling
sight in this working-class
district. However the
church burnt down in 1723.
Restored, it was again badly
damaged by fire on May 17,
1990. Since then it has been
magnificently restored and
reconsecrated. Standing in
the middle of the garden-
cemetery, it is worth the visit.

★ **Fjällgatan (F** D2**)**
'Mountain Street' has been
a popular viewpoint since
the 17th century. In those
days people often strolled
past Stigberget where the
city's executions took place.
As a tribute to the much-
loved Stockholm writer
Per Anders Fogelström

(1917–98) part of the
belvedere terrace is
named after him.

★ **Kåkar (F** D2**)**
There is in Vitabergsparken,
around Sofia Kyrka, a
cluster of old red-painted
wooden houses (*kåkar*): it
is a remnant of Stockholm's
oldest working-class
dwellings. They illustrate
the crowded living
conditions which were
once typical in Söder.

★ **Fåfängan (F** F2**)**
→ *Tel. 642 99 00*
Daily 11am–8pm
Another spot from where
the views are spectacular,
both in the direction of
the city and across to
Djurgården and the sea-

approach to Stockholm.
The name is derived from
the old custom of calling
land which was no good
for agriculture, *fåfäng* or
'vain', and allowing people
to erect gazebos and the
like on it. One such gazebo,
built by the merchant
Fredrik Lundin in 1770,
is now a coffee house.

★ **Koloniområden (F** B4**)**
→ *Approx. 1.5 miles from*
Skanstull subway station
In the past, allotments
used to provide poorer
city-dwellers with a
chance to grow their
own vegetables. Today
they provide a calm green
space for the stressed
city workers.

Transportation and hotels in Stockholm

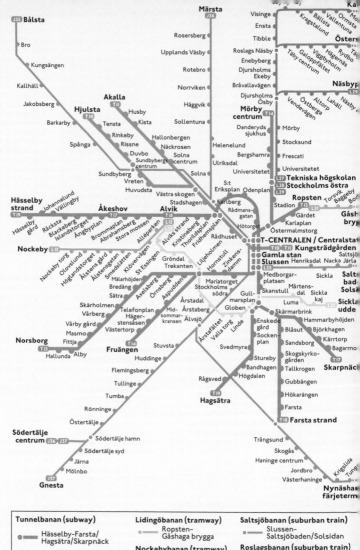

Tunnelbanan (subway)
- Hässelby-Farsta/Hagsätra/Skarpnäck
- Mörby centrum/Ropsten-Fruängen/Norsborg
- Akalla/Hjulsta-Kungsträdgården

Lidingöbanan (tramway)
- Ropsten-Gåshaga brygga

Nockebybanan (tramway)
- Alvik-Nockeby

Tvärbanan (tramway)
- Alvik-Sickla udde

Saltsjöbanan (suburban train)
- Slussen-Saltsjöbaden/Solsidan

Roslagsbanan (suburban train)
- Stockholms östra-Näsbypark/Österskär/Kårsta

Pendeltåg (suburban train)
- Bålsta/Märsta-Nynäshamn/Södertälje/Gnesta

Streets

af Pontins väg **E** D3
Alkärret **E** B2
Allhelgonagatan **F** B-C3
Allmänna gränd **E** B3
Almlöfsgatan **B** A1
Alsnögatan **F** F2
Amiralsvägen **B** C4
Andréegatan **E** C3
Ankargränd **A** D2
Apelbergsgatan **C** D2
Arkivgatan **A** C2
Armfeltsgatan **D** B1-C1
Arsenalsgatan **B** A1-2
Artilerigatan
 B B1, **C** F2-3, **D** A3-B1
Askrikegatan **D** C1
Assessorsgatan **F** B3
Atlasgatan **C** A2
Atlasmuren **C** A2
Ångströmsgatan **C** A2
Åsögatan **F** B-E2
Ångskärsgatan **D** C1-2
Baggensgatan **A** E3, **B** A4
Banérgatan **B** D1, **D** B4-C3
Bangårdsgången **F** B2
Bankkajen **A** D2
Barnhusbron **C** B2-3
Barnhusgatan **C** C-D2
Barnängsgatan **F** E2-3
Bastugatan **A** B-C4, **F** A1
Beckholmsvägen **E** C3
Beckholmsbron **E** C3-4
Bedoirsgränd **A** D3
Bellmans väg **E** E3-F2
Bellmansgatan
 A C4, **F** A1-B2
Bellmansroporten **E** E2
Bengt Ekehjelmsgatan **F** A2
Bergsgatan **C** A3-B3
Biblioteksgatan **C** E2-E3
Birger Jarlsgatan
 B A1, **C** D1-F3
Birger Jarlstorg **A** C2, **C** D3
Birkagatan **C** A1
Bjurholmsgatan **F** C3
Bjurholmsplan **F** C-D3
Björngårdsgatan **F** A1-B2
Blanchegatan **D** C1-1
Blasieholmsgatan
 B A2, **C** F3
Blasieholmstorg **B** A2
Blecktornsgränd **A** C4
Blecktornsstigen **F** D3
Blekholmsgatan **C** C3
Blekholmsstranden **C** C3

Blekholmsterrassen **C** C3
Blekholmstunneln **C** C3
Blekingegatan **F** C3
Bo Bergmans gata **D** B1
Bohusgatan **F** C-D4
Bolinders plan **C** C3
Bollhusgränd **A** E2, **B** A4
Bollnästorget **E** D2
Bondegatan **F** C-E2
Borgmästargatan **F** D2
Brahegatan **C** F1-2, **D** A2
Brantingsgatan **D** C-D1
Breda gatan **E** C3
Bredgränd **A** E-F2, **B** A4
Breitenfeltsgatan **D** C2
Brunkebergstorg **C** E3
Brunkebergstunneln **C** E2
Brunnsgatan **C** E2
Brunnsgränd **A** E-F2, **B** A4
Bryggargatan **C** D3
Bråvallagatan **C** A2
Brännerigatan **F** C3
Brännkyrkagatan
 A C-D4, **F** A-B1
Bältgatan **D** B2
Carl Alberts gränd **F** B2
Carl-Gustav Lindstedts
 gata **C** B2-3
Celsiusgatan **C** A3
Centralbron **A** B1-D3, **C** D4
Centralplan **C** D3
Didrick Ficks gränd **A** D2
Dag Hammarskjölds väg
 D D3-4
Dalagatan **C** B1-2
Dalslandsgatan **F** C3
Danderydsgatan **C** E1
Danderydsplan **C** E1
Danvikstull **F** F2
De Geersgatan **D** C1-2
Djurgårdsbron **D** C4, **E** B1
Djurgårdsbrunnsvägen
 D E-F3
Djurgårdsslätten **E** C3
Djurgårdstrand **E** B3
Djurgårdsvägen
 D C4, **E** B1-F3
Drakens gränd **A** E-F3, **B** A4
Drottning Sofias väg **D** A1
Drottninggatan
 A C-D1, **C** C1-D3
Duvnäsgatan **F** E2
Döbelnsgatan **C** D1-2

Dörjgränd **F** D4
Engelbrektsgatan **C** E1-E2
Erik Dahlbergsgatan
 D B2-C1
Eriksbergsgatan **C** E1
Eriksbergsplan **C** E1
Eriksdalsgatan **F** B4
Erstagatan **F** E2
Evert Taubes terrass **C** D4
Exercisplan **B** C4
Falkenbergsgatan **E** B2-3
Fatburs Brunnsgata **F** A-B2
Fatburs Kvarngata **F** A2
Fatbursgatan **F** A-B2
Ferkens gränd **A** E-F3, **B** A4
Fjällgatan **F** D1-2
Flaggmansvägen **B** B-C4
Flemminggatan **C** A2-B3
Floragatan **C** F1
Folke Bernadottes väg
 D E-F4, **E** E-F1
Folkungagatan **F** B2-F2
Fredrikshovsgatan **D** C3-4
Fredsgatan **A** C-D1, **C** D4-E3
Frejgatan **C** B1
Funckensgränd **A** E3
Furusundsgatan **D** C-D1
Färgargårdstorget **F** E3
Färgarplan **F** E3
G. Hälsinges gränd **A** D2
Gaffelgränd **A** F3, **B** A4
Galärvarvsvägen **D** C4, **E** B1
Gamla Brogatan **C** D3
Gamla Lundagatan **A** A4
Garvargatan **C** B4
Gaveliusgatan **F** E3
Gillögagatan **D** C1
Glasbruksgatan **F** C1
Glasbruksklippan **F** C-D1
Gotlandsgatan **F** C-D3
Greta Garbos torg **F** C-D3
Grev Magnigatan
 B C-D1, **D** B3-4
Grev Turegatan
 C F1-2, **D** A2-3
Greve von Essens väg
 D E2-F3
Grevgatan **B** C1, **D** A4-B2
Grevgränd **B** A2, **C** E-F3
Grindsgatan **F** B3
Grubbens gata **C** A2
Grubbensringen **B** 2-3
Gruvbacken **F** E2
Gräsgatan **F** B4
Guldfjärdsplan **A** D4, **F** B1
Guldfjärdsterrassen **A** D4

Guldgränd **A** D4, **F** B1
Gumshornsgatan **D** B3
Gustav Adolfs torg **A** D1, **C** E3
Gustav III:s staty **A** F2, **B** A3
Gyllenstiernsgatan **D** D2-3
Gymnasiegränd **A** C3
Gåsgränd **A** D2
Gärdesgatan **D** D-F3
Gästrikegatan **C** A1
Göran Hälsinges gränd **A** D2
Götgatan **F** B1-C3
Hallandsgatan **F** B3
Hammarby Kajväg **F** D4
Hammarbyvägen **F** D-E4
Hammargatan **C** E1
Hamngatan **B** A1, **C** E3
Hantverkargatan **C** A3-B3
Havregatan **F** B3-4
Hazeliusbacken **F** D3
Hazeliusporten **E** B-C2
Helga Lekamens gränd **A** D2
Helgagatan **F** B3
Herkulesgatan **C** B3
Hjärnegatan **C** B3
Holländargatan **C** C1-D2
Holmamiralens torg **B** C4
Holmamiralens väg **B** C4
Hornsgatan **A** D4, **F** A-B1
Hovslagargatan
 A F1, **B** A-B2, **C** F3, **D** A4
Humlegårdsgatan **C** E-F2
Hälsingegatan **C** B1
Högbergsgatan **F** A2-C1
Klarastrandsleden **A** C2-3
Klaratunneln **C** D-E3
Klefbecks backe **F** D2-E3
Klippgatan **F** D2
Kocksgatan **F** C2
Kommendörsgatan
 C F2, **D** A2
Kornhamnstorg **A** E3
Korphoppsgränd **F** F4
Kronobergsgatan **C** A2-3
Krukmakargatan **F** A1
Kråkgränd **A** E-F2, **B** A4
Kungsbron **C** C2
Kungsbroplan **C** C3
Kungsbrostrand **C** C3
Kungsgatan **C** B3-E2
Kungsholms hamnplan **C** B4
Kungsholms kyrkoplan **C** C3
Kungsholms strand **C** A-B2
Kungsholms strandstig **C** B2
Kungsholmsgatan **C** A-C3
Kungsholmstorg **C** B4
Kungsklippan **C** B3

Kungstensgatan **C** C-D1
Kungsträdgårdsgatan **C** E3
Kvarngatan **F** B1-2
Kyrkslingan **B** B-C4
Kåkbrinken **A** D3
Källargränd **A** E2
Kölnavägen **F** F4
Köpmangatan **A** E2
Köpmantorget **A** E2, **B** A4
Laboratoriegatan **D** D4
Lagerhusgränd **D** E1
Lehusens gränd **F** A2-3
Lejonbacken **A** D-E2
Lejonslätten **E** B1
Lejonstedts gränd **A** D-E3
Lidingövägen **D** A-B1
Lilla Hoparegränd
 A E-F3, **B** A4
Lilla Mejtens gränd **F** D-E3
Lilla Nygatan **A** D2-3
Lindarängsvägen **D** D-F2
Linnégatan **C** F2, **D** A-C3
Livryttarstigen **D** C1
Ljustergränd **F** D4
Ljusterögatan **F** E3
Lodgatan **C** E1
Londonviadukten **F** E2
Lotsgatan **F** E2
Lovisagatan **D** C3-4
Ludvigsbergsgatan **A** A4
Lugnets allé **F** F4
Lumavägen **F** E4
Luntmakargatan **C** D1-2
Lusthusporten **D** C4, **E** B1
Lützengatan **D** C2
Långa gatan **E** C3
Långa raden **B** C-D4
Lästmakargatan **C** E2
Löjtnantsgatan **D** B1
Magnus Ladulåsgatan
 F A3-B2
Majorsgatan **C** F2, **D** A3
Malmgårdsvägen **F** D-E3
Malmskillnadsgatan
 C D2-E3
Malmvägen **D** E-F1
Maria Prästgårdsgata **F** A2
Maria Trappgränd **A** D4
Mariatorget **F** A1
Markvardsgatan **C** C-D1
Masthamnen **F** F2
Medborgarplatsen **F** B2
Metargatan **F** D3
Mjärdgränd **F** D4
Monteliusvägen **A** B4, **F** A1
Mosebacke torg **F** C1
Munkbrogatan **A** D3
Munkbrohamnen **A** D3
Munkbroleden **A** D-E3
Munkbron **A** D2
Museikajen **B** B3
Museispårväg
 B B-C1, **D** A-B4

Muselvägen **D** F4
Myntgatan **A** D2, **C** E4
Mälarrampen **A** E4
Mälartorget **A** D3
Mäster Pers gränd **F** D2-3
Mårten Trotzigs gränd **A** E3
Mäster Samuelsgatan
 C D-E3
Nackagatan **F** E-F3
Narvavägen **D** B3-C4
Nils Ferlins torg **C** D3
Nobelgatan **D** D4, **E** C-D1
Noe Arksgränd **F** B2
Nordenskiöldsgatan **E** C3
Norr Mälarstrand **A** C-A4
Norra Agnegatan **C** B3
Norra Bankogränd
 A E3, **B** A5
Norra Bantorget **C** C2
Norra Brobänken **B** B3
Norra Dryckesgränd
 A E3, **B** A5
Norra Hammarbyhamnen
 F E3-4
Norra Helgeandstrappan
 A D1
Norra Järnvägsbron **A** B1-C2
Norra Riddarholmshamnen
 A C2
Norra Varvsporten **E** B1
Norrbackagatan **C** A2
Norrbro **A** D1-E1, **C** E4
Norrlandsgatan **C** E2-E3
Norrmalmstorg **B** A1, **C** E3
Norrtullsgatan **C** C1
Nybergsgatan **D** B3
Nybrogatan
 B A1, **C** F1-3, **D** A2-3
Nybrohamnen **B** A-B1
Nybrokajen
 B A-B2, **C** F3, **D** A4
Nybroplan **B** A1, **C** F3
Nygränd **A** E-F2, **B** A4
Nytorget **F** D2-3
Nytorgsgatan **F** C1-D2
Näckströmsgatan **B** A1
Närkesgatan **F** D3
Nätgränd **F** D4
Observatoriegatan **C** B-C1
Odengatan **C** B-D1
Odenplan **C** C1
Olaus Petrigatan **D** B-C1
Olof Palmes gata **C** C-D2
Olofsgatan **C** D2
Orangerivägen **E** E-F2
Oxenstiernsgatan **D** D3
Ölandsgatan **F** C3
Öresundsgatan **D** E1
Örlogsvägen **B** D5, **E** A3
Österlånggatan
 A E2-3, **B** A4-5, **C** E4
Östermalmsgatan
 C E-F1, **D** A-B2

Östermalmstorg **C** F2, **D** A3
Östgötagatan **F** C2-4
Östhammarsgatan **D** E1
Östra Brobänken **B** C3, **E** A3
Östra Järnvägsgatan **C** C3
Östra Slussgatan **E** A4
Östra terrassrampen **A** E4
Östra Varvsgatan **E** C3
Överskärargränd **A** D2
Packhusgränd **A** E-F3, **B** A5
Parkgatan **C** A3
Parmmätargatan **C** B3-4
Pelikangränd **A** E-F3, **B** A4
Pilgatan **C** A4
Pipersgatan **C** B3
Ploggatan **F** E2
Polhems tvärgränd **C** A2
Polhemsgatan **C** A3-4
Pontonjärgatan **C** A4
Prins Eugens väg **E** E-F3
Pryssgränd **A** C4, **F** A-B1
Prästgatan **A** D2-E3
Pustegränd **A** D4, **F** B1
Ragnar Östbergs plan
 A A1-2, **C** A4
Raoul Wallenbergs torg
 C F3
Rapsgatan **F** A3-4
Regeringsgatan **C** E2-3
Rehnsgatan **C** D1
Renstiernas gata **F** D1-3
Repslagargatan **F** B1-2
Riddargatan **B** B1-D1,
 C F2-3, **D** A3-C4
Riddarholmsbron **A** C2
Riddarhusgränd **A** C-D2
Riddarhustorget **A** C2-3
Rigagatan **D** B2
Riksbron **A** D1
Riksgatan **A** D1-2
Riksplan **A** D1
Rimbogatan **C** E2
Rindögatan **D** C-D1
Ringvägen **F** A-D3
Rosendalsterrassen **E** E2
Rosendalsvägen
 D D-F4, **E** D1-F2
Runebergsgatan **C** E1
Runebergsplan **C** E1
Rutger Fuchsgatan **F** C3-4
Ryssgården **F** B1
Ryssviksvägen **E** E3
Rådhusgränd **A** D2
Rådmansgatan **C** C2-E1
Råggatan **F** B3-4
Räntmästartrappan **A** F4
Rödbodgatan **A** C1
Rödbodtorget **A** C1
Rökubbsgatan **D** E1
Rörstrandsgatan **C** A1
Sachsgatan **F** A3
Saltmätargatan **C** D1-2
Saltsjörampen **A** E4

Salviigränd **A** D2
Samuel Owens gata **C** C4
Sandelsgatan **D** B-C1
Sandhamnsgatan **D** E1-2
Sankt Eriksbron **C** A2
Sankt Eriksgatan **C** A1
Sankt Eriksplan **C** A2
Sankt Paulsgatan **F** A2-B1
Scheelegatan **C** B3
Schering Rosenhanes
 gränd **A** C2
Schönfeldts gränd **A** D3
Sehlstedtsgatan **D** E2
Serafimerstranden
 A A1, **C** C3-4
Sergelgatan **C** D3
Sergels torg **C** D3
Siargatan **F** B2-3
Sibyllegatan
 C F2-3, **D** A3-B1
Sickla kaj **F** F4
Sigtunagatan **C** B1
Singelbacken **E** D-E3
Sirishovsvägen **E** E2-3
Sjukhusbacken **F** A3
Själagårdsgatan **A** E-F2
Sjöbergsplan **A** E4, **F** B1
Skansbrogatan **F** C4
Skansbropåfarten **F** C4
Skanstullsbron **F** C4
Skaraborgsgatan **F** B1-2
Skarpögatan **D** D-E3
Skeppar Karls gränd
 A E-F2, **B** A4
Skeppargatan
 B B1, **D** A4-B2
Skeppsbrokajen
 A F3, **B** A4-5
Skeppsbron
 A F3, **B** A5, **C** F4
Skeppsholmsbron
 B B3, **C** F4
Skillinggränd **C** C4
Skolgränd **A** C4
Skomakargatan **A** E2-3
Skottgränd **A** E-F2, **B** A4
Skräddargränd **A** D3
Skånegatan **F** C3-E2
Slottsbacken **A** E2, **B** A3
Slottskajen **A** D2-E1, **C** E4
Slupskjulsvägen **B** C3
Slussplan **A** E4
Slussterrassen **A** E4
Slöjdgatan **C** D3
Smålandsgatan **C** E3
Snickarbacken **C** E2
Sofiagatan **F** D3
Solgränd **A** D-E2
Sollidsbacken **E** D3
Sollidsporten **E** D3
Spektens gränd **A** D2
Spelbomskans torg **C** C1
Stadsgårdshamnen **F** C-D1